C000052249

The Rest of Life

The Rest of Life

REST, PLAY, EATING, STUDYING, SEX
FROM A KINGDOM PERSPECTIVE

Ben Witherington III

William B. Eerdmans Publishing Company

Grand Rapids, Michigan / Cambridge, U.K.

© 2012 Ben Witherington III
All rights reserved

Published 2012 by
Wm. B. Eerdmans Publishing Co.
2140 Oak Industrial Drive N.E., Grand Rapids, Michigan 49505 /
P.O. Box 163, Cambridge CB3 9PU U.K.

Printed in the United States of America

18 17 16 15 14 13 12   7 6 5 4 3 2 1

Library of Congress Cataloging-in-Publication Data

Witherington, Ben, 1951-
The rest of life: rest, play, eating, studying, sex from a kingdom perspective /
 Ben Witherington III.
  p.   cm.
 ISBN 978-0-8028-6737-7 (pbk.: alk. paper)
 1. Christian life.   I. Title.

BV4501.3.W575   2012
248.4 — dc23

2012004723

www.eerdmans.com

Contents

Introduction

In this little series of Kingdom reflection studies we have already covered the Kingdom itself in *Imminent Domain*, worship from a Kingdom perspective in *We Have Seen His Glory*, money and material possessions in *Jesus and Money*,[1] and most recently work from a Kingdom perspective in *Work*. But what about the rest of the normal life of a Christian? The concern of this series has been with the normal weekly events in the normal Christian life — work, rest, play, worship, spending, study, eating, relating. The thing that has struck me in doing this series is (1) how little serious theological and ethical reflection has been given to what some might call mundane existence, and (2) how even less consideration has been given to the interrelationship of these normal weekly Christian activities.

Should we be striving for some sort of balance, some sort of equilibrium between these various factors, like eating a balanced diet? Does that balance vary from Christian to Christian? Should Christian life normally involve all of these factors in the normal given week? These are the sort of considerations you too seldom hear anything about in tomes on the theology and ethics of the Bible. Oh yes, we have endless volumes on sexual relationships

---

1. Brazos, 2010. The other books in the series are with Eerdmans.

prompted by our sex-obsessed age, but most of them tell us little about how sex should relate to the rest of social interaction in a normal Christian life. The big picture is missing. And even worse, the subject is discussed with no reference whatsoever to the eschatological situation, the Kingdom situation that we have been in since Jesus first came.

Do we really think we can simply ignore the ongoing reign and rule of God, the ongoing divine intervention and salvation of God in and for the world and its effect on day-to-day Christian life, and say anything lasting or meaningful about work, rest, play, worship, etc.? I for one do not think so. I think that we have too often abstracted these discussions from the larger theological and ethical matrix in which they ought to be discussed. Let's consider, just as a teaser, a particular passage of Scripture — a few verses of 1 Corinthians 7. Here is what Paul says to us about normal life, including marriage, in verses 29-31:

> What I mean, brothers and sisters, is that the time has been shortened. From now on those who have wives should live as if they did not; those who mourn, as if they did not; those who are happy, as if they were not; those who buy something, as if it were not theirs to keep; those who use the things of the world, as if not engrossed in them. For this world in its present form is passing away.

The artful dodge sometimes taken around this passage is to say, "Well Paul, bless his heart, thought Christ was surely returning during his lifetime, and so of course he spoke this way, but with the benefit of 2,000 years of hindsight we know he was wrong." But Paul says nothing whatsoever about the future coming of Christ in this passage. He is talking about an eschatological change *already set in motion* such that the "schema" of the world is already passing away, and the time has been shortened, in some way. The eschatological wheels are already turning and they are already affecting normal daily life for Christians, the form of things like life and death, buying and selling, marrying and giving in marriage. The earthly givens are passing away.

So Paul calls us to have a very different perspective on work, rest, play, eating, worship, relating, marrying, studying, mourning, and so on. He characterizes that perspective as one of detachment — we should live "as if not." He even says this about Christian marriage! From his point of view, almost none of these *normal* earthly activities are eternal, not even marriage (see for example Rom. 7:1-5, where he says that the wife is freed from the law of the husband when he dies). Work, rest, play, study, eating, marrying, and giving in marriage will come and go as the Kingdom dawns. They were part of our tasks and ways of relating in this life in this world in this age. But not in the age to come. Only worshiping and relating seem to endure when faith becomes sight and hope is finally realized and love endures, so that we finally love God and neighbor as we ought. As I have stressed in this series, what Paul and other New Testament writers call us to is to live in the light of the future, live in the light of the Kingdom that has come, is coming, and shall come, letting our eschatological worldview shape how we view and should live out all the normal activities of a Christian life.

Now I grant that this is a radical perspective. It is frankly not one that most modern Christians embrace, or indeed, even *know* they ought to embrace. But in this series I am saying we at the cusp of the twenty-first century must embrace this perspective. It is not the job of the church to baptize the status quo of "normal life" and call it good. It is not our job to merely hallow the ordinary. It is our task to follow Paul and other New Testament writers, and have an extraordinary perspective on the ordinary — a Kingdom perspective.

In this penultimate study in our series, we intend to cover in more detail those topics that we have only mentioned in passing in previous studies in this series, beginning with the whole cluster of ideas focused on matters of rest, Sabbath, retirement, sleep, restoration, and even sabbaticals. Our study, then, will begin with the distaff side of the work-rest tandem. Let's get to work, so we can understand "rest" from a Kingdom perspective, because as the Master said, "The night comes when no one can work."

Pentecost 2011

CHAPTER ONE

Is There a Sabbatical Plan for Christians?

The Sabbath . . . means togetherness instead of separation, per-manence instead of transience, continuity instead of disruption, and presence instead of absence.

Sigve Tonstad

The debate began with the earliest Christians. Paul and the Judaizers had all sorts of struggles over the issue of how much of the Mosaic covenant should be applied to the followers of Christ. Should they all be circumcised, even the Gentiles? Should they keep the Jewish Sabbath? What about the food laws? Paul, for his part, and the author of Hebrews as well, believed that covenants and their strictures were package deals. As Paul says plainly in Galatians 3–4, if you allow yourself to be circumcised, taking on the oath sign of the Mosaic covenant, then you are obligated to keep all 600+ commandments given on Moses' watch. His basic advice to all his converts was — Don't go there. Indeed, as we shall see, he urged that Christians should not be enmeshed in observing Jewish festivals (new moons, Sabbaths) any more than they were obligated to get themselves circumcised. The new covenant had a new set of rules, and what was confusing was that some of the old rules were carried over into the new covenant, but most were not — especially not the boundary-defining rules about circumcision, Sabbath, and food.

Since there has been a Sabbath controversy in the church since almost Day One of its existence, it behooves us to look at this matter closely, but we need to be aware that Sabbath talk is part of the larger dialogue in Scripture about rest, sleep, restoration, Jubilee, and a cluster of related topics. In this chapter we will be conversing with a crucial recent study on these matters — Sigve Tonstad's *The Lost Meaning of the Seventh Day*.

I am not interesting in getting involved in the sometimes rancorous debate as to whether the Lord's Day is the Christian Sabbath or not. (I don't think the New Testament supports such an equation of the two. I do think that the Lord's Day is the appropriate day of Christian worship in light of Easter.) I am interested in Christians having an adequate theology of rest, whether it involves the Sabbath or not. But we must, however, engage the debate as to whether Adventist practice of the Sabbath is what *all* Christians should follow, as this sort of globalizing theology of rest can lead not merely to contention, but ironically enough to a short-circuiting of the larger and more meaningful discussion of a theology of rest.

Lost and Found — Sabbath and Seventh Day

It is the thesis of S. K. Tonstad, in his well-written and wide-ranging study titled *The Lost Meaning of the Seventh Day,* that the majority of Christendom needs to resurrect and recover the observance of the seventh day, the Sabbath.[1] His concern is, however, not just with the loss of a "day of rest" or a particular ritual pat-

---

1. S. K. Tonstad, *The Lost Meaning of the Seventh Day* (Berrien Springs, MI: Andrews University Press, 2009), p. xi. In the rest of this chapter, page numbers in parentheses in the text refer to this book.

tern to the Christian week, but with theology — "The character of the seventh day is misconstrued if it is seen as a national or religious marker of identity and not as a theological statement. To the extent that it is a part of God's story, it cannot be suppressed indefinitely. It must reassert itself to complete its God-ordained mission; it cannot remain permanently in exile" (p. 5). That Tonstad uses strong language in his study is understandable. He is an ardent Seventh Day Adventist, and he clearly has a "dog in this fight" as we would say in North Carolina.

As might be expected, the author will address the seventh day in the Old Testament, the seventh day in the New Testament, and postbiblical issues raised by the eclipse of the seventh day, issues such as the alienation between Christians and Jews, the estrangement of Christians from the material world, and the loss of understanding of the theological depth of the seventh-day observance. It is clear that the author sees the eclipse of seventh-day observance as one of the direct causes of some of these problems.

For Tonstad's case, much hangs on his reading of Genesis 2:1-3, and as one reads his exposition of this text, one begins to see where the argument will go. He says, "By the act of hallowing the seventh day God drives the stake of divine presence into the soil of human time" (p. 21). This sentence is characteristic of the rhetoric of this book, which abounds in potent metaphorical images. And here is where we begin to see some of the oddity of the case he wants to make. What Genesis 2:1-3 says is that God *ceased* (*shabbat*) from creating. In other words, the seventh day is when he was *not* actively involved in doing some creative work in his material creation. The text suggests something more like God sitting back and enjoying what he had just accomplished and seeing that it was very good. The seventh day *itself* is not the capstone of *creation*. If anything deserves that title it is the creation of woman last of all creatures. Rather, the seventh day is the day when one takes time to appreciate the creation already finished. And it is this day that God both blessed and hallowed.

The absence of divine creative activity is not the same thing as divine presence.

And what exactly does it mean to say God finished his work on the seventh day? Does it mean he created this day especially and set it apart from all other days? This statement in Genesis has always been puzzled over, and it led in fact in the Septuagint (or LXX) version of Genesis 2:1-3 to the translation that God finished his creative work on the *sixth* day! The work in question, however, cannot be the day itself, since the Hebrew says he finished it "*on* that day." The activity in view must surely be his blessing and hallowing of the day, not a further act of creation.

Blessing and hallowing, while not a materially creative work, can nonetheless be said to be an activity. And perhaps it might be well to remember that when it comes to that, Jesus said that God is *always* working, in some sense (John 5:17). To cease from creating is not the same as to cease from all activity. And finally, the text does not say "and God said let there be a seventh day, and lo there was a seventh day." The seventh day is not a special creation of God. Indeed, one could argue that the seventh day is still ongoing, as God has still ceased from his inaugural creation work, and in Genesis 2:1-3 there is no statement saying "there was evening and morning, a seventh day."

Tonstad rejects the usually scholarly logic that Sabbath observance was something that came into play in the Exodus tradition, and should be distinguished from the seventh day of creation material in Genesis 2, preferring unitive readings of Genesis following older Jewish scholars such as U. Cassuto and N. Sarna. He thinks the Documentary Hypothesis has run out of literary gas. In his view, the Sabbath must be seen as an ordinance of creation for all time — all this deduced from Genesis 2:1-3. The net effect of this hermeneutical move is that the Sabbath and its observance rest on all humankind; it is not a rite set up for God's chosen people, Israel, alone.

One of the problems with a good active theological mind that works synthetically, as Tonstad's does, is that it tends to overread texts, by which I mean it reads more theology into a text than is there. Tonstad, for example, wants to see the seventh day, and God's benediction on the seventh day, as not merely a retrospective evaluation of the goodness of God's creative work, but prospective of redemption. He suggests that the "orientation of the seventh day from the beginning oscillates between memory and hope, between the reality of Paradise Lost and the prospect of Paradise Regained; the oscillation of hope is stronger than the oscillation of memory. In its original configuration, the seventh day must be seen as promise as much as memorial. It forecasts that God's 'very good' will be sustained, transforming the human experience into a journey of hope" (p. 59).

Unfortunately, as the British would say, this is "over-egging the pudding." Genesis 2:1-3 is clearly retrospective, not prospective; it does not in itself promise anything about the future, nor does it establish a particular pattern of Sabbath observance. That clearly comes later, when there is a people, Israel, to do such observing. That is not to deny the connection between the seventh day in Genesis and the later Israelite worship pattern; the latter definitely is grounded in the former, but the two are not the same. The seventh day is God's celebration of his own creative work, and since God is not a narcissist, understandably nothing is said about worship, or even creatures needing to worship the creator God, at that juncture. As Tonstad admits, there is only one text in Genesis that deals with the seventh day and its theology, Genesis 2:1-3, and there is frankly no attempt there to connect that to a remedy for what happens afterwards, namely the Fall.

As is well known, Paul connects the new covenant with the Abrahamic covenant, in distinction from the Mosaic covenant (Galatians 3–4), and thus it becomes important for Tonstad that somehow he connect Abraham to Sabbath observance and the Sabbath commandment. His attempt to do this is weak, because the most he can muster is the fact that Abraham is said to keep some commandments of God, though there is no evidence whatsoever that he kept the Sabbath. It is entirely an argument from silence to suggest Abraham was a sabbatarian, and indeed Paul's distinctions between the Abrahamic and Mosaic covenants should have warned us against such a reading of the Abraham story.

To a real extent, a person's theology of rest is going to be determined or affected, at least, by his or her theology of work. If work is seen as a curse, then rest is seen as an inherent blessing, and so the two are viewed as reciprocal. But there is a problem with this whole perspective, as I have shown in the earlier books in this Kingdom series.[2] The problem is twofold: (1) worship is not necessarily the same thing as rest, and (2) work is not a curse. The inauguration of the Sabbath day (Exodus 16) is an attempt to get Israel to once more focus on the worship of the one true God after years when there had been nothing but slavery and work. With freedom came the opportunity and obligation to worship, and God set up for them a weekly practice that involved rest from other activities, but not from worshiping God.

Tonstad makes much of the fact that the Exodus 16 text says that God remembered his promises to Abraham. Indeed, he did, but he did not promise Abraham, Isaac, or Jacob a Sabbath observance, nor is there any hint they observed such a day in Genesis. He promised them a relationship, a homeland, descendants, and some freedom from oppression. Now we learn in Exodus 16 that the most important part of the freedom was freedom to continue cultivating that deep relationship with God, freedom to worship, and Exodus 19:4 says that God had not merely delivered Israel but "brought you to myself." The real goal was more a promised relationship than a promised land. Or better said, it was both, with the emphasis on the promised ongoing relationship.

2. See especially *Work: A Kingdom Perspective* and also *We Have Seen His Glory: A Kingdom Perspective on Worship* (both published by Eerdmans, 2011 and 2010 respectively).

The Rest of Life

Close examination of Exodus 31:13-17 reveals that the Sabbath pattern is a sign between God and Israel, a perpetual covenant between God and Israel, a reminder that it is God who hallows and sanctifies things, including his own people. Nothing is said or suggested here about such a covenant with humankind in general, or that God had made such a covenant with all of humankind before the Exodus-Sinai events. Remembering the sabbatical pattern of God's creation is one thing, and remembering a previous ordinance to observe a Sabbath by a people is another; Exodus does not ask Israel to remember such a previous ordinance, it asks them to remember God's creation pattern, and God's covenant faithfulness with the patriarchs — a different matter.

What fallen people, who endure suffering, sin, and sorrow, disease, decay, and death, need far more than rest and restoration is resurrection, which makes them immune to all the effects of fallenness. And whereas the retrospective old pattern of liberation focused on a day of rest and restoration, and thereby of renewal of a personal relationship and worship, what the new pattern of liberation focused on was *not* the old sort of redemption, a mere freedom from, but a new sort of redemption and salvation that enabled a freedom to.

Worship in light of the eschaton is not worship that makes allowances or is a response to the Fall with its breaking of the relationship with God. Worship in the light of the eschaton is worship in spirit and in truth whenever and wherever. It does not require a holy spot (Mt. Zion), nor does it require a holy day, for all days in the eschatological view are holy unto the Lord. Eschatological worship looks forward to not merely when we will study war no more, but when there will be no more night. New heaven and new earth are not a mere continuation of a sabbatical pattern, they are the completion of a new covenant with humankind, the fulfillment of the promise of Easter and the first resurrection, the raising of Jesus.

There is a reason why there is no temple in the new creation, and it is because there is no division between sacred and secular days, zones, or places anymore, something Jesus announced in John 4 already. Paul foresees all this clearly when he says that while some observe one particular day unto the Lord, others see all days as the Lord's days, and he thinks they are right. He thinks we shouldn't insist on anyone observing a Sabbath day anymore, not because he has given up on rest, restoration, or worship, but because since the resurrection of Jesus we are now looking forward to a time when all days are hallowed. The sabbatical pattern is a pattern for God's people in a fallen world, a world where there is night, where there is need for rest, where work is never done, never completely finished. It is not a pattern from or for the eschaton, where there is no night, no need for rest, and work is complete in various senses.

The question is whether Christian worship and life should be patterned on the Kingdom that is still to come, or on the original old creation pattern, whether Christian worship and life should be about new life, resurrection life in Christ, or the old birth, the old creation, the old creatureliness, the old need for rest and restoration. My answer is, we are not under the old creation, old covenant mandate anymore. We are under a new covenant mandate and we should daily remind ourselves, "If anyone is in Christ there is already a new creation." The Sabbath mandate is for those who have been born, and in particular for those in Mosaic covenant with God. The new creation, new worship mandate is for those who have been born again of water and Spirit, who live out of the future and not primarily out of the past. They live out of the eighth-day Easter morning, and not the seventh, the close of the old creation workweek.

Were Adam and Eve, before the Fall, given a commandment to keep the seventh day holy? No. Their only commandment was to stay away from the tree of the knowledge of good and evil. Was toilsomeness in work due to a fallen creation said to be something inherent in the nature of work, or was it said to be part of the curse on the ground due to the Fall? The latter is true, and *rest* in that context becomes relief from the effects of the Fall on work, not part of the original creation mandate.

One of the interesting ideas in Tonstad's book is that the Sabbath is a sign like a flag is a sign. I would say that actually it's a symbol — something that participates in the reality to which it points. It points to God's ceasing from his creative activity, and as such when Israel does the same they participate in such ceasing from creative activity. Just as people react violently in the U.S. to flag burning, so Exodus says death is the penalty for violating the Sabbath, as it is sacred.

Another interesting idea is the relationship of Sabbath observance and creation keeping and care. One of the more important aspects to Sabbath law is that it has concern for those most vulnerable and heavy laden — the beast of burden, the slave, the resident alien (Exod. 20:10; Deut. 5:12-15). It prioritizes from the bottom up not the top down, with most concern for those who most need rest (pp. 126-27). Tonstad calls the Sabbath year and the year of Jubilee "Sabbath satellites" that extend the pattern of rest to debt and the need of the land for rest.

Isaiah 56:4-5 foresees a day when eunuchs and strangers who keep the Sabbath and hold fast the covenant will be given a place within God's house and an everlasting name, a name better than sons and daughters. Isaiah's vision is about those who choose to do this, and so it goes beyond the ethnic view of a people. Instead of an ethnic group we have a confessing community.

Isaiah 66:23 suggests that when new creation rolls around it will involve new moons and Sabbaths. But what it actually says is that all flesh shall come to worship before God, from new moon to new moon, from Sabbath to Sabbath. Isaiah develops a Sabbath ideology that goes beyond Israel into an eschatological situation involving everyone. He has the last word about Sabbath in the Old Testament, not Nehemiah or later Old Testament developments. And this vision of the end, when lion lies down with lamb, involves the demise of the serpent — he will bite the dust (Isa. 65:25). Tonstad eloquently puts it this way: "The serpent who at the beginning bit the fruit of the tree of knowledge will, in the end, bite the dust" (p. 157).

For Tonstad's case to work, namely that the Sabbath is for all people all the time, and not just specifically for Jews, he must marginalize texts like Nehemiah 13:3 and maximize Isaiah 56–66, for Nehemiah separates Israel from those of foreign descent. Tonstad is forced to admit that the subsequent history of the Sabbath observance moves more along Nehemiah's lines than Isaiah's vision (pp. 167-68). Nehemiah suggests to Tonstad an approach involving exclusion and coercion, something he sees continued with the Pharisees and Jewish officials in the Gospels (Matt. 12:2; Mark 2:24; Luke 6:2; John 5:16). Attempts to dilute Jewish distinctiveness and distinctive praxis are seen as threats to the national and ethnic identity (cf. 1 Macc. 1:1-61; 2:42). According to Tonstad, Pharisees were believers in coercion. A perceived attack on Sabbath observance was seen as an attack on exclusive Jewish existence, excluding Gentiles. Sabbath observance was seen as an essential feature of Jewish identity. The evidence that this was the early Jewish view, and that they read the Pentateuch to say that the Sabbath was set up for the Hebrew people, is clear in various kinds of early Jewish literatures. For example, consider the following two quotes:

Rabbi Levi: "If Israel kept the Sabbath properly even for one day, the son of David would come. Why? Because it is equivalent to all the commandments" (Exodus Rabbah 25:12).

Rabbi Johanan in the name of Simeon ben Tochai said: "If Israel were to keep two Sabbaths according to the laws thereof, they would be redeemed immediately" (B. T. Shabb. 118b). It is Israel that is called to keep the Sabbath and will see the benefits if they do so.

It is precisely into this sort of context and this sort of exclusivistic conversation about the Sabbath that Jesus interjects himself in a provocative way. Why all these healings on the Sabbath, even nonemergency healings on the Sabbath? Are they deliberate provocations? Is Jesus redefining work? Is Jesus redefining Sabbath and what it means to cease from work? And why the vociferous objections to such healings in all the layers of the gospel tradition? One of the things that becomes clear in John 5 is that the identity of Jesus is revealed and wrapped up in these Sabbath healings. John 5:17-18 says, "My Father is working and I am working," and this amounts to a claim to equality with God, even in terms of what should and shouldn't happen on the Sabbath. Jesus' opponent is not really, or not in the main, "the Jews," that is, Jewish officials; it is Satan, the father of lies (pp. 182ff.).

Does Jesus break the Sabbath by all his healings on that day, or repristinate its original meaning and intent by doing so? Does he break the Pharisaic conception of the Sabbath and what it must entail? Tonstad sees Jesus' "it is finished" in John 19 as an allusion to the Genesis 2:1-2 reference to when God finished creating. On the cross and by Jesus' death the finishing of the correcting what is wrong has happened, just as at creation the finishing of what was right and good has happened. The new creation begins with the death of Jesus, when the new covenant is cut, the sacrifice offered, the cutting off of the old self happens (p. 200).

Reading Jesus in light of Paul (Gal. 5:14), Tonstad argues that Christ has brought the Law to completion in one sentence, namely love your neighbor as yourself, in that on the cross he fulfilled and completed that commandment, and so the Law ceases to be a way of righteousness or a way to fulfill all righteousness, as Christ has already completed the task. The Sabbath is the designated day for the liberation of creation, according to Tonstad (pp. 214-18).

By binding or combining the first two commandments into one, Jesus is in effect rejecting any interpretation of Sabbath observance that does not involve and incorporate love of neighbor. The Sabbath, then, is the pledge of God's healing, restoring presence. The Sabbath was made for us, not the other way around. While we were made for God, the Sabbath by contrast was made as a blessing for all of us. And when its observance involves the avoidance of restoring and healing and blessing and loving one's neighbor, it is not a proper Sabbath observance at all (p. 220).

Obviously, the real litmus test, if not *bête noir,* for Tonstad's case to hold water, is his rereading and reinterpreting of some of the things Paul says. So as he turns to Paul he first makes a hermeneutical move to do damage control in advance. "The message of Jesus in the Gospels, addressing all Christians in an open-ended readership, takes precedence, and the voice of Paul, addressing specific situations in named churches, will not dilute or invalidate the Gospel narrative. Applying this insight to the Sabbath, we should be reluctant to accept that the affirmation of the Sabbath that we find in the Gospels will be disaffirmed by Paul in his letters" (p. 227).

Clearly, Galatians becomes something of a real trial for Tonstad's kind of interpretation, and so it is not a surprise that he must expend considerable energy trying to explain away some of the things Paul does say. Following Troy Martin, he wants to take the reference in Galatians 4:8-11 to turning back to paganism, not to turning to circumcision and Judaism, and so the reference to days and months and seasons and years becomes a Pauline critique of the pagan religious calendar (p. 231)! The scenario, then, is that Gentiles in Galatia, put off by the Judaizers, are prepared to even give up on the Pauline form of Christianity and go native, back to paganism and the elemental spirits of the universe.

Unfortunately for this theory, it crashes to earth with a thud in Paul's allegory in which he contrasts two *Jewish* covenants — the Abrahamic one and the Mosaic one, and urges his audience to cast out the Judaizers who were wooing them, and to reject circumcision, and indeed to embrace the new covenant which is linked to the Abrahamic covenant, not the Mosaic one. One of the singular failures of Tonstad's book is that it really doesn't come to grips with the theology of new covenant in the New Testament, which is not simply a renewal of the old covenant. This is especially the case in Galatians 2, where Paul upbraids a fellow Jewish Christian, Peter, for turning back to kosher food observance rather than dining with Gentiles in Galatia. The demand for circumcision in Paul's mind implies an observance of all the Mosaic commandments, including Sabbath-keeping, and Paul will have none of this.

So what sort of strategy does Tonstad pursue to marginalize the normal reading of Paul? We take a dose of Louis Martyn's apocalyptic reading of Paul's letter to the Galatians, sprinkle in a reminder that what matters most for Paul is story, narrative, not so much doctrine and commandments, and remind the audience that, after all, most of Galatians is polemics and hyperbolic rhetoric. Following Richard Hays's interpretation of *pistis Christou* (the faithfulness of Christ), Tonstad sees the issue in Galatians as God's setting right what has gone wrong in the world by sending Jesus — it is the faithfulness of Christ, then, that is set over against Law, which was incapable of setting a fallen world to rights.

Consider the following quotes from Tonstad's book: "Paul eschews exclusion but not particularity; he decries discrimination but not differences" (p. 243). "Galatians may tell us what Paul thinks about the Sabbath in the context of the activity of his opponents, but it is not thereby representative of what Paul thinks about the Sabbath or even the best place to launch such an inquiry" (p. 247). Paul is not rejecting Sabbath observance, but he "chips away at the ethnocentric disposition of Judaism and its sociology of exclusion." The seventh day is seen as God's commitment to all human beings — a statement of God for the whole human family, not the preserve of Jews (p. 248).

Following Graham Stanton, Tonstad concludes that "the law of Christ" mentioned in Galatians refers to the example of Christ's life and Christ's teachings, and what Christ's teachings involve is the law of Moses redefined by Christ with the love command and the bearing of each other's burdens as its essence, and it is fulfilled by Christ in his own self-giving love, especially on the cross (p. 250). The difficulty is, Tonstad is right on some aspects of his analysis of Paul, but wrong on the key questions of Sabbath and covenants.

If Galatians is a major hurdle on the way to rescuing the Sabbath for Christian use, Colossians 2:16 would seem to be the brick wall that stops all forward motion in such a quest. So this text must be explained in one of several peculiar ways by Tonstad: (1) it does not refer to the seventh-day Sabbath, or (2) it does refer to the Sabbath, but Paul, *mirabile dictu,* is affirming the Colossians Sabbath observance rather than decrying it, or (3) *sabbata* here refers to Sabbaths that have lost their Jewish character (p. 259). One attempt at exegetical gymnastics is to suggest that while the phrase "festivals, new moons, Sabbaths" may well allude to Hosea 2:11, the Sabbath in question was not the weekly Sabbath but rather the annual cultic Sabbath of the liturgical calendar (Lev. 16:31) (p. 262).

Following Troy Martin (again) he argues that the key text means "Don't let anyone judge you in regard to your ongoing praxis of festivals, new moons, Sabbaths, but just make sure that in doing those things you discern the body of Christ by and in these practices" (pp. 264-65). Paul, then, would be reassuring the Colossians that such praxis is fine, and he is protecting them from Cynic polemics against such Jewish praxis. The problem with this view is that when we run into phrases like "the worship of angels," the context and content of Paul's *own critique* of the Colossians has to do with the allure of Judaism, including Jewish worship praxis in various forms.

One of the things Tonstad finds incredible is the idea that Paul might link together pagan philosophy and religion on the one hand and Mosaic religion on the other under the heading of *stoicheia.* Was Paul fighting on two fronts? The answer is yes in fact, and *stoicheia* means elementary teachings that one should be *beyond* and leaving in the past if you are a Christian. Following Clint Arnold, Tonstad suggests that Paul is critiquing some sort of syncretistic gumbo that involves some Jewish elements, and some pagan elements. Even if so, the Jewish elements he chose to single out for critique included the Jewish religious calendar in a general way — new moons and Sabbaths included (p. 267).

For Tonstad it is inconceivable that while the Creator may have one special day, the Redeemer might have or set up another — one day the sign of creation, the other day the sign of redemption (p. 274). Inconceivable, unless there has been a breach in the identity of God, especially in light of how Christ the Redeemer in Colossians is also portrayed as the creator as well. If restoration proclaims the faithfulness of God to the original promises, then one should expect, according to Tonstad, the Sabbath to be reaffirmed in the new creation. "In Colossians as a whole, the *sabbata* do not come straight from the OT or from a simple Judaizing opponent" (p. 274). This totally ignores the sapiential character of the language here, in which Wisdom alongside of Yahweh is involved in the creation of the universe, not Wisdom as Yahweh. The Creator and the Redeemer are not *the same person;* the Son is a different person than the Father, though with the Father he shares the fullness of the *pleroma,* the divine essence or substance.

The last explicit mention of the Sabbath in the New Testament is in Hebrews — its theme is that there remains a Sabbath rest for God's people (Heb. 4:9). Tonstad suggests that the Sabbath that remains refers to a Sabbath that can now be enjoyed by Christians and celebrated by Christians, even though the "rest" that the author has in mind has not yet come to fruition and in fact awaits the return of Christ. What is most odd about this part of Tonstad's argument is that we hear not one word about the fact that the audience for this sermon is probably Jewish Christians tempted to go in a retrograde motion back into Judaism. There is not even a peep about the obsolescence language in Hebrews or the "better than" language when it comes to the Mosaic covenant and its inauguration of Sabbath observance. For Tonstad, Sabbath proclaims the faithfulness of God, his reliability.

Having taken up the challenge of showing that the Bible favors sabbatarianism for one and all, Tonstad then still has a huge task before him, to which he devotes several chapters: How then did it happen that the church abandoned the Sabbath for the Lord's Day or replaced the former with the latter, or subsumed the former into the latter? How could that happen if God expected of all creatures great and small a perpetual Sabbath praxis (pp. 298ff.)?

Despite sporadic evidence of continued Sabbath observance by Christians into the fourth century, perhaps principally by folk like the Ebionites, and in places like Syria, Ethiopia, and Egypt, Tonstad admits that from the middle of the second century A.D., the trend is lopsidedly in favor of Sunday rather than Sabbath observance (p. 301). Tonstad notes that the second-century theologians don't debate whether Sabbath should be kept or not; the praxis just slips into oblivion and no one can say exactly when Sunday worship began. Actually we *can* say: it is mentioned in the New Testament, and it is reaffirmed by early second-century theologians.

Justin Martyr is quite clear — we observe Sunday because not only is it the day God began to create the world, it is the day Jesus rose from the dead (First Apology 67). But even clearer and earlier is the pronouncement of Ignatius of Antioch to the Magnesians: "Those who were brought up in the ancient order of things have come to the possession of a new hope, no longer observing the Sabbath, but living in the observance of the Lord's Day, on which our life has sprung up again by Him and by His death" (Mag. 9:1). Tonstad will put this down to waning Jewish influence in and on the church, alongside of rising anti-Semitism as well. In his view, the parting of the ways led to the parting of the days.

Tonstad even suggests Sunday observance was something Christians borrowed from Mithraism or from the cult of Sol Invictus (pp. 308-14). There is a straight repudiation, without evidence, of Oscar Cullmann's assertion that Sunday is a specifically Christian festival day (p. 309). And he follows Jürgen Moltmann's suggestion that widespread Sunday observance came by royal decree of Constantine on March 3, A.D. 312, when he urged all judges, townspeople, and all occupations to rest on the honorable day of the sun. This can be called Adventist polemics, since there is already evidence not only in Ignatius and Justin, but in the pagan writer Pliny (who refers to Christians on the first day of a week singing songs to Christ as to a God at dawn), that long before Constantine in the province of Asia, Bithynia, Syria, and elsewhere Christians were worshiping on Sunday.

The likely reality is that when a large number of Gentiles became Christian through the Pauline and other missions — Gentiles who had had no synagogue connections previously — Christian worship outside the context of Sabbath observance happened, and this was not critiqued by Paul or his co-workers, only by the Judaizers from Jerusalem. There is no evidence at all that mixed Jew and Gentile congregations in Ephesus or Corinth or Philippi continued to observe the Sabbath as part of their Christian praxis, though undoubtedly various Jewish Christians and God-fearers probably continued to go to the synagogue.

Tonstad, in chapter 17, suggests that anti-Judaism must be put down as a main reason for the eclipse of Sabbath praxis among Christians, but another is Hellenism, more particularly Platonism with its devaluation of the material world and the human body, which is seen as a prison house of the immortal soul, and so on (pp. 316ff.). The early church imbibes and adopts a Platonic worldview without seeing its incompatibility with a biblical doctrine of the goodness of creation, of matter, of bodies, of resurrection. The revised Platonic gospel promises escape from creation into a disembodied heaven, not the transformation of creation.

On these terms, it is hard to explain why highly Hellenized Diaspora Jews would continue to observe a Sabbath, continue to affirm the body, bodily life, and even a doctrine of resurrection as a litmus test of sorts after A.D. 70. *The answer is that a theology of Sabbath is not the same as a theology of creation, though the former is linked to, and to some extent grounded in, the latter. One can have a perfectly robust theology of Sabbath-keeping, and a deficient theology of creation, or a robust creation theology, with no theology of Sabbath at all, as Genesis as a whole does not affirm, much less mandate, Sabbath-keeping, and Genesis 2:1-3 doesn't say God instructed his human creatures to do so.*

A theology that sees no immortal virtue in the body is a theology that can justify its neglect or abuse. And Tonstad suggests that Platonic medieval Christianity aided and abetted things like the Black Plague because medicinal research was not seen as essential to life or very important, and studying the human body itself was seen as a sacrilege (pp. 332-38). "The medieval idea of the body and the earth had a paralyzing impact because it did not offer any incentive to improve people's lot in this life" (p. 336).

A case is made by Tonstad for the ecological potency of Sabbath observance. "Neglect of creation and a relentless anti-sabbatarian bias are constants in the Christian enterprise" (p. 395). In fact Christians are often the worst offenders against creation, the worst exploiters. It is not a biblical idea to say that nature serves no purpose but to serve the needs and whims of humans. The problem with Tonstad's argument here is that it does not go far enough in an eschatological direction. The earth is not merely crying out "Give it a rest," it is crying out "We need an extreme makeover, a rejuvenation, a new creation," and Sabbath is not about that. Sabbath is not about resurrection, it's about ceasing from creative activity. Look, for example, at Romans 8:20 — "the creation awaits the revealing of the sons of God," which is to say it awaits our resurrection and its own. It does not await a Sabbath rest; it awaits a resurrection. One of the oddest parts in this whole book is Tonstad's discussion of Romans 8, with no mention at all of resurrection (pp. 396-98). But this is in part based on his faulty reading of the Isaianic background here. He takes Isaiah

66:22-23 to mean that in the new creation we will be observing new moons and Sabbaths. But what that text actually suggests is that in the new creation we will worship throughout the liturgical calendar. Notice, for example, how the quote of this text in Revelation 15:4 leaves out the reference to Sabbath and new moons quite deliberately. That's because the author already knows of *another* day of worship — see Revelation 1 — "the Lord's day."

Perhaps a part of the problem is a misconceiving of resurrection itself. Tonstad seems to think resurrection involves creation ex nihilo, even though Paul says it involves transformation of the living, and one would also assume raising of the dead bits of those who still have remains (pp. 412ff.). He places much stress on the "instantaneous" nature of the change, at odds with the long-process thinking of science about change. It is well to mention that one can overdo the analogy between old creation and new creation in various ways. Tonstad appears to be a materialist as well, by which I mean he seems to think death means extinction despite texts like 2 Corinthians 5 — absent from the body and present with the Lord.

The temptation to blame Constantine and his ongoing legacy is strong, as Tonstad is forced to admit that church history after Constantine does not largely support his views. The Council of Laodicea legislated against Sabbath observance and other Judaizing practices in 360. The Council of Trent in 1566 said that the church of God in its wisdom decided that the celebration of the Sabbath should be transferred to Sunday. Eusebius, bishop of Caesarea, sometime before 339 when he died, when commenting on Psalm 92 (91 in the LXX), said, "[A]ll that was prescribed for the Sabbath we have transferred to the Lord's Day, inasmuch as it is the most important, the one which dominates, the first and the one which has more value than the Sabbath of the Jews."[3] The Council of Trent simply said that all the rest of the Decalogue is

3. Patrologia graeca 23:1172.

reinforced as it is part of natural law, but the Sabbath is not. The Sabbath is seen as not fixed but rather alterable and subject to change. The Sabbath then should be seen as an example of ceremonial law. Aquinas believed a day of rest does belong to what can be called natural law, but not the designation of a specific day. Calvin calls the Sabbath "a time-bound application of a timeless principle." The major objection seems to be the arbitrariness of designating a particular day, and this by Calvin and Luther who revel in the notion of God's sovereignty and right to be arbitrary. But Tonstad counters that it is not arbitrariness but rather God's love for and faithfulness to his creation and creatures that explains the Sabbath (pp. 426-40).

When he gets down to attacking Constantine, Tonstad is at his most polemical: "The emperor rules by decree, not by persuasion, he governs by command, not by consent; he relies on force, not on consensus or popular acclaim. The relationship between the emperor and his subjects is that of master and subject, the former issuing orders and the latter obeying them. There is no built-in mechanism of accountability in the imperial system of government except for riots and assassinations" (p. 446). Constantine said, "What higher duty have I in virtue of my imperial office and policy than to dissipate errors and repress rash indiscretions and so to cause all to offer to Almighty God true religion, honest concord and due worship?" (p. 448). The church in turn adopted the imperial structure of the empire right down to the *pontifex maximus* term while the empire was busy making Christianity its official religion and imposing it on all. What Tonstad is most concerned with is the effect of this marriage of theology and empire (God began to be portrayed as the ultimate despot and the ultimate Emperor, whom the human emperor modeled himself on). The church assigned to God the attributes that belonged exclusively to Caesar (pp. 450ff.). As quickly becomes apparent, the polemic is not just against Constantine but against the church he helped bring out of the shadows of persecution and out of the underground and into the mainstream of the Greco-Roman world. Here a large dose of Peter Leithart's fine recent study, *Defending Constantine*,[4] could have helped correct some of the misstatements and overstatements in this part of Tonstad's study.

There is no denying Tonstad's passion and eloquence when it comes to the subject of the Sabbath: "The Sabbath brings a message of togetherness instead of separation, permanence instead of transience, God's presence instead of God's absence, freedom instead of subjugation, continuity instead of discontinuity, wholeness instead of disintegration, other-centeredness instead of arbitrariness, and divine narrative more than divine imperative" (p. 515). But good rhetoric does not necessarily come from good exegesis or good analysis of good exegesis, and in the end, the New Testament itself proves Tonstad wrong about the necessity of Christian sabbatarian praxis.

At the very beginning of this stimulating book a personal story is told, a story of Sigve Tonstad growing up in Norway and of how the one day of the week that was special in terms of food and fellowship in an otherwise rather Spartan week was the Sabbath. In some ways, this very revealing story reminded me of the beginning of *Citizen Kane* and the "rosebud" story. It explains a good deal of why Tonstad has so vigorously and zealously defended the Sabbath at such great length in this well-written book. It is because he does not want to give up on something so precious, so vital, so valuable, so meaningful to him ever since his childhood. He is to be commended for such loyalty to a biblical principle, as it is all too rare these days. But the good (and Sabbath is a good) can get in the way of seeing and embracing the best, the *summum bonum,* and that is what has happened in this wide-ranging defense of the Sabbath.

What eclipses the seventh day, according to New Testament theology, is the *eighth day,* and its observance. The day of the week

4. Downers Grove, IL: InterVarsity, 2010.

God began the first creation (Sunday) is the day he began it again. He began the new creation in the resurrection of Jesus. And what God's people need far more than rest or even restoration is resurrection — for when one rises from the dead, one finally shakes off the weariness of the old fallen mortal flesh and needs, and studies Sabbath no more.

Thus, while we live in this vale of tears and will continue to need rest, there is something we need far more, which is far better — resurrection. Christians are an Easter people, a people called to live into and toward our own resurrection, grounded in the resurrection of Jesus. Christian worship praxis should be based not on the Mosaic Sabbath praxis, not even on the old creation seventh-day praxis, but on the new creation praxis, which signals where God and his people are going, not merely where they have been.

In the already and not-yet of Kingdom come, celebrating the Lord's Day is the way Christians live into a future that will one day come when the kingdoms of this world become the kingdoms of our Lord. The Lord's Day celebration is the way we affirm that the future is as bright as the promises of God. The old creation rest was good, but it was only a foretaste of glory divine; like Melchizedek, it foreshadowed something greater that was to come. The Lord's Day is the flag Jesus planted in the ground one April morning in A.D. 30. It is the one that Christians should wave and cheer, now and evermore, for it is the ensign of our own future — "for we shall be made like him," even in our flesh. The attributes of Sabbath were not transferred to the Lord's Day; they were transcended by the Lord's Day.

The Debate Rages On — Give It a Rest?

It should be apparent from what has already been said in this chapter that Sabbath observance and recognizing a need for rest are not one and the same thing. In fact, if we did a study of Hebrews 3–4 we would note that even the biblical author distinguishes *kata-pausis* from *sabbatismos*. According to Hebrews, there is a rest prepared for all of us, and it has to do with God's rest. In this second portion of the chapter we will discuss rest both mundane and eschatological, and will stress that what we say about the latter should norm how we view, approach, implement the former.

It is not necessary for me to stress that all human beings need rest, indeed need it every single day. And there is a difference between necessary rest and pure laziness. We are all familiar with the stock character from Wisdom literature — the sluggard. One of the characterizations of this figure reads as follows — "How long will you lie there, O sluggard? When will you arise from your sleep? A little slumber, a little sleep, a little folding of the hands to rest and poverty will come upon you like a bandit, and want like an armed man" (Prov. 6:9-10). What is interesting about this quotation is that it distinguishes sleep from rest, and so should we. To say that human beings need rest is not the same as saying they need sleep. Both things are true, sleep being the deepest form of rest presumably. So let us revise what I said in the first sentence of this paragraph — we need both rest and sleep.

Not long ago I read a rather frightening report about people whose work involves an enormous mental component — I am talking about thinkers, writers, philosophers, ponderers, and the like. I am talking about people like me. What is frightening is that the study said that persons who use some 40 percent+ of their calories for brain work are likely to need far more rest and sleep than persons who do manual labor — carpenters, stonemasons, landscapers, etc. I believe this. I have two good friends who are New Testament scholars. Both of them suffered from chronic brain fatigue in their fifties. One retired early. The other had to cut back even though he was just a research professor. They couldn't read for any length of time, and couldn't concentrate on any detailed or complicated matters. It was very frustrating. What I learned from watching them go through this is that sleep is one thing, rest is another, and we need both. We can't just work all the time even when we are doing something we very much love. It doesn't work that way. The normal life cycle requires more than work and sleep. It also requires rest.

But we should have been able to figure this out from examining what is said about God in Genesis 1–2. God never sleeps. But God did cease from his creation activities. He did in some sense rest, and the author of Hebrews will tell us that we have a chance to participate in God's rest. We will say more about this in a moment, but it would be well to discuss first what the Bible says about sleep itself, both literally and metaphorically, so our distinctions between sleep and rest will be sharper, clearer.

The very first reference to sleep in the Bible is in the story of Adam himself. Genesis 2:21 tells us that God caused a deep sleep to come over Adam, in this case for the purpose of not-so-minor surgery — to form Eve from one of his ribs. Psalm 127:2 should be compared — "in vain do you rise early and stay up late, toiling for food to eat — for he gives his loved ones sleep." Sleep may be natural, but it's also a gift from God. A colleague of mine has sleep apnea, which makes sleep hard to come by. This is on the opposite end of the spectrum from John Wesley, who said that one of the keys to the Methodist revival was that not only could he sleep on his horse while riding to his next appointment, but at night he could bid sleep to come, and it would. If only. . . . My suggestion would be that since (1) all of life is a gift from God, and (2) this includes both what seems natural and daily to us and that which seems serendipitous and out of the ordinary, that we should see rest and sleep as gifts from God and not just assume it is what happens to us when we are too tired to continue working, studying, eating, playing, or a myriad of other conscious activities.

Figuring out your own personal limits, how much rest and sleep you as an individual need, is not something one can generalize about. Yes, most humans need about seven hours of sleep a

night. But it is a moving target. Those who are recovering from ill-
ness or injury or surgery need considerably more so the body can
concentrate on healing, and not on other functions. And aging
comes into the picture as well. The older you get, the more rest
you need as the body wears out and wears down. Rather than simply thinking of this from a mundane point of view, I would suggest we need to think in light of not only the fact that life is a gift,
but also that our bodies are "temples of the Holy Spirit," places
where the sacred dwells. We have an inherent obligation to take
care of our mortal frame and use it wisely so that we may be good
servants of God. Rest and sleep are essential for all waking tasks,
including specifically ministerial ones.

I have seen what dealing with one crisis after another does to
ministers. We call it burnout. The old Methodists used to ask the
question at their annual conference — "Who are the worn-out
preachers?" By this was meant, who can no longer fully function
and itinerate as a Methodist circuit rider? Whether one is a circuit
rider or a located minister, good health and a rested body are keys
to doing one's best for the Lord. What is interesting about the discussion of rest in the New Testament is that according to the author of Hebrews, we will experience God's rest in the life to come.
One might expect that we wouldn't need rest in the life to come.
Not so, at least in the sense of experiencing the complete wellness
and wholeness and holiness that God always intended for us. And
yes, we will lay down our burdens and experience rest in that
sense in the life to come as well. But we need to consider more
closely what the author of Hebrews says about rest.

The author of Hebrews is not talking about taking a day off,
or sleeping, or sabbatarian practice. He is talking about entering
God's rest, and according to Hebrews 4:3 the key to having done so
is believing. Neither Moses, who never entered the promised land,
nor even Joshua, who did enter the land but did not give the people of God rest (indeed he gave them war), ushered God's people
into *God's* rest, *even though* Moses had ushered them into the

practice of the Sabbath. For the Christian the question becomes not merely, how can I get better rest, but will I enter God's rest? But what in the world is Hebrews 4:3-11 about? Is the author talking about R.I.P. — entering God's rest and heaven at death? Or is he talking about something eschatological? Let us pause for a minute to reflect on what Hebrews tells us about rest from a theological perspective in this passage.

First, what should we make of Hebrews 4:3? Here we certainly have a present-tense verb: "For we who have believed enter into rest." F. F. Bruce wants to see this as a generalizing present — "[E]ntry into that rest is for us who have believed."[5] On this showing the rest is purely future and presumably to be identified with the heavenly resting place, which in due course will also descend to earth. The Psalm quote makes clear this is God's rest first and foremost, and it is something God has in fact been enjoying since the end of his work of creation. The LXX of Psalm 95 uses the term *katapausis,* and we will find it in Hebrews 3:11, 18; 4:1, 3 (twice), 5, and 10-11; the verbal cognate is used in the intransitive twice, 4:4, 4:10, and in the transitive at 4:8. Since our author does not specifically define what he means by this term, we must assume it was already understandable to his audience.

The more usual term for "rest" in the LXX and New Testament is *anapausis;* thus our author is specifically drawing on the terminology of Psalm 95, but also on Genesis 2:2, where in the LXX we also have the verbal form of this same word, *katapauo.* In the LXX *katapausis* can mean either a state of rest or a resting place — six times it is used in the latter sense, four times in the former. In Psalm 95:11 it could refer to either. What might favor the idea of a resting place in Psalm 95 is that the worshiper is invited to enter the temple (i.e., the earthly resting place or sanctuary of God). Again, the warning example of the wilderness-wandering generation is in regard to entering the promised land

5. F. F. Bruce, *Hebrews* (Grand Rapids: Eerdmans, 1990), pp. 106-8.

— a resting place. The point is that both the land and the temple as the resting place could be described by this word *katapausis*.

It is clear that the primary reference must be to a place: in Psalm 95, the alternative to entering into God's rest is falling dead in the desert. In Deuteronomy 12:9 also we hear of the land as a resting place. But we must at this juncture go beyond the Old Testament. We know that in Jewish intertestamental exposition Psalm 95 was linked to an eschatological resting place, so much so that some rabbis called the New Jerusalem God's resting place. Also in the intertestamental literature, Psalm 95:11 was used to refer to the eschatological resting place of the elect, a heavenly place entered at death (cf. Joseph and Asenath 7–9). Our writer is certainly familiar with this idea and probably is referring to an eschatological resting place, also associated with a heavenly land (11:14ff.) or the heavenly city (11:10), or the heavenly sanctuary (6:19ff.). This idea is probably confirmed when later in this homily our author is going to stress that the heavenly sanctuary is where God is now resting, where some of the saints now are, and where Christ is the high priest.

But this rest is something God entered at creation. The land of Canaan in fact is a mere type of the true rest of God, as is the temple. By juxtaposing Psalm 95 and Genesis 2:2, the whole purpose of creation and redemption is juxtaposed. On this showing God's rest is the climax of the creation story, not the creation of humanity. More importantly, our author has used the word *sabbatismos* at 4:9. The verb *sabbatizo* in the LXX means "to keep the Sabbath"; the noun literally would mean Sabbath-keeping. Thus, when at verse 9 our author refers to a Sabbath that remains, presumably he means the same thing he said earlier when he said there remained a Sabbath rest, though we could translate it "there remains a celebration of the Sabbath for God's people."

The idea of a day of rest is then seen as yet another type on earth of God's ultimate rest — which means not so much an absence of activity, though that is a component, but the presence of joy, a sense of fulfillment and completion (we may compare the idea of perfection at this point). It is also clear from 4:11 that our author sees this rest as a future condition/event even for Christians, for they are to strive to enter that rest still, and disbelief (*apistia*) and disobedience (*apatheia*) can disqualify them. Even this rest is only fully in heaven now, but our author will elsewhere say (at 12:22) that we have already come to the heavenly Jerusalem. In Hebrews 11 we should bear in mind that faith is defined as a present assurance about or grasp on the future truth — a truth that, while it exists in heaven now, will one day appear more fully on earth. Thus it is quite possible that by using the term "today" our author means to convey the idea that the audience has a foretaste of this rest, just as they have in part realized the benefits of salvation, for they are already partakers in Christ. It is, in short, possible that the rest, like salvation, is already/not yet. At 4:8 we are reminded that Joshua, even though he entered the land, did not in fact give the people rest, for the promise is renewed later in Psalm 95.

Andrew Lincoln, putting all this together, suggests that we emulate God by ceasing from our (dead) works and by exercising faith in the promises (cf. 6:1, 9:14).[6] Dead works are those that do not, but might be thought to, contribute to our salvation. Our author doesn't in fact talk about works righteousness as does Paul, and justification by faith is not a big issue in Hebrews. The author is concerned with pointless works, not works righteousness.

It may be that the Jewish Christian audience assumed that by some particular Jewish form of Sabbath observance they might enhance their chance to enter the rest of God. The author of Hebrews appears to deny this. It should be borne in mind that as far as we can tell, the church very early on assumed the practice of observing a new special day for Christ — the Lord's Day, celebrating the resurrection (see Rev. 1:10). Thus it is unlikely that our author is saying that even Jewish Christians now have a rest by keep-

6. In his delivered lectures on Hebrews at Gordon-Conwell Seminary.

ing the Sabbath. More likely what he means is the audience has a rest here and now by living by faith in Christ, and ceasing from dead works. They like God are to cease from works that no longer need to be undertaken. They are to appreciate the rest they have in Christ, the shalom they have in him. By redemption they have entered a foretaste of the final rest of God — a rest from sin, the fear of death, etc. The point is that they have this foretaste of rest in part now, to the extent that salvation is already present. But it will only be consummated later, either when they enter the heavenly city at death or at the eschaton. The rest affirmed here for the Jewish Christian audience is not different from the rest available to Gentile believers as well.

When we begin to think about "rest" the way the author of Hebrews does, we begin to realize that there is ordinary rest and then there is "Rest" in the theological sense, and the latter should be norming the way we think about the former. What I mean by this is, for example, that having the peace that comes from the living presence of Christ in one's life gives one rest from worry about salvation (and so freedom from thinking one needs to do this or that to secure salvation), or worry about one's final destination, or anxiety about whether one's life matters or not. This sort of mental and emotional and spiritual rest comes not from Sabbath observance but from relationship with Christ. In addition, the rest one has in Christ alleviates the need to maintain Mosaic ritual practices such as Sabbath observance.

The ordinary rest we need, and hopefully get every day, reminds us that we are mortal and frail and are not yet in our resurrection bodies. Indeed, we are living in a condition that is rightly characterized by Paul as "outwardly wasting away. . . ." The older we get, the easier we tire, the more we need our rest. But this very condition should daily remind us that we are being prepared for a better rest, a bigger rest, indeed for God's rest. The ordinary rest reminds us of the extraordinary one we have only a foretaste of now, but will fully enjoy later when Kingdom comes.

The interesting thing is that when we die, our bodies no longer need rest in the mundane sense. It is ironic that we put R.I.P. on gravestones of Christians. Christians haven't lain down to pleasant dreams; they have gone on into the living presence of God and have become much more alive, indeed eternally so. Nor are the saints snoozing in the afterlife. There is no doctrine of soul sleep in the New Testament, as we shall see in a moment (see, e.g., Revelation 6, where the saints under the altar in heaven are awake and anxious to get on to the next phase of things). Bodily rest now foreshadows a resurrection body that will not need rest later. It does not foreshadow rest in heaven, if we mean actual physical rest. Yes, in heaven there apparently isn't a to-do list. But no, we are not lounging around in the afterlife. We are worshiping God and enjoying him forever.

What does the Bible say about sleep, as distinguished from rest? Let us start with the theological use of the term "sleep" in the New Testament. There were metaphorical phrases in the Old Testament about sleeping with or being gathered to one's ancestors once one died. But the term "sleep" means more than being deceased in the New Testament. Consider, for example, three texts — the story of Jairus's daughter in Mark 5 (see especially v. 39), or the story of Lazarus in John 11 (see especially the first ten verses), or the discussion about the dead in 1 Thessalonians 4:13-18. In all three of these texts the subject is people who are actually dead. Their deaths, however, are viewed in light of their coming resurrection from the dead — in the case of Jairus's daughter and Lazarus this transpires during the ministry of Jesus; in the case of the Thessalonians, this is viewed as happening when Christ returns. It is Christ in all cases who causes resurrection. Why then call death "sleep"? Because the speaker in each case knows that the dead will return from death like someone returns from a good night's sleep — refreshed, renewed, awake, and able to take nourishment. The term "sleep" in early Jewish literature does not refer to the condition of the dead, but to the fact that they are not permanently dead. This leads to a brief comment on "soul sleep," the notion that the dead in Christ sleep until the second coming.

It can be said unequivocally that there is nothing in the Bible to commend the theory of soul sleep. The New Testament writers in the first place do not affirm the Greco-Roman notion of the immortal soul, nor should we. These writers are, almost without exception, Jews, and they aren't as Hellenized in their views as say Philo was. They are, however, also not monists or materialists, by which I mean that they do believe there is a nonmaterial part of the human makeup, regularly called the human spirit. So, for example, on the cross in Luke's Gospel Jesus commends his "spirit" unto God as he dies. Or Paul, in 2 Corinthians 5, can talk about the deceased Christian as a person being absent from the body, but present with the Lord. While there is no body/soul dichotomy in the New Testament, there is a limited dualism between body and the rest of the person, such that when believers die their personality, their spirit, the immaterial part of them, goes to be with God. This is affirmed not merely by Jesus (see the parable of the rich man and Lazarus in Luke 16), but also by Paul, and for that matter by John of Patmos, who talks about seeing the martyred saints in heaven wide awake and complaining "How long, O Lord?" in Revelation 6. What all this means is that the term "sleep" is only applied to the dead in a loose sense — they appear, from a purely earthbound and mundane point of view, to be sleeping in the ground, but in fact they are alive and aware and awake in the presence of God; and they will one day inhabit a better body as well, a resurrection body. Sleep prefigures death, to be sure, but when it comes to the death of the faithful, they have nothing to fear.

When we think of sleep in the more mundane sense, we are reminded of the line in *Macbeth:* "Sleep that knits up the raveled sleeve of care," the kind of sleep known as "the best medicine." Shakespeare knew what he was talking about. Sleep is a good stress and anxiety buster, and all of us need it daily, some more badly than others. Some people are apt to see sleeping as a waste of a third of our lives. The Bible knows nothing of such a workaholic point of view. It sees sleep as restorative, health-giving and life-giving in various ways. It has been said that we should give a third of our lives to sleeping so we can give the other two thirds to active and vital and vigorous service to God. Let us reflect for a moment on the traditional child's prayer — "Now I lay me down to sleep, I pray the Lord my soul to keep. If I should die before I wake, I pray the Lord my soul to take." Sometimes the second sentence reads "Keep me safe all through the night and wake me with the morning light." What this simple prayer recognizes is that one loses control over one's life for the duration of time that one is asleep. So the prayer is about protection from harm when one is so vulnerable, and in a sense it is also about keeping short accounts with God. In effect it says, "If something untoward happens to me while I am sleeping, please take me to yourself, Lord," thereby making peace with God each night as one turns out the light.

Sabbath and rest and sleep are important theological topics, requiring careful theological reflection and careful distinctions as this chapter demonstrates, but there are a couple of other related topics we should consider at this juncture. Let's consider the modern secular notion of retirement. As I said in my book titled *Work*, you will find plenty in the Bible about rest and sleep, but nothing whatsoever about the notion of retirement, at say sixty-five, from one's lifelong vocation. John Wesley prayed until almost the day he died in 1791 — "Lord, don't let me live to be useless." That would be my prayer as well. In fact, the notion of retirement, at whatever age, is basically a modern, Western, industrialized-nation, post–World War II idea. And in fact in many cases, it's a very bad idea. I can hardly tell you the number of ministers I have known who have died only months after "retirement." You cannot tell me this had nothing to do with the fact that many of them felt they were no longer contributing members of society, never mind

God's kingdom. Moltmann has some crucial insights of relevance to this topic:

> Christian eschatology has never thought of the end of history as a kind of retirement or payday or accomplished purpose but has regarded it totally without purpose as a hymn of praise for unending joy, as an ever-varying round dance of the redeemed in the Trinitarian fullness of God, and as the complete harmony of soul and body. It has not hoped for an unearthly heaven of bodiless souls but for a new body penetrated by the spirit and redeemed from the bondage of law and death. . . . Christian eschatology has painted the end of history in the colors of aesthetic categories.[7]

I should stress that I have no problems with people who "retire" from what they call their "secular" jobs in order to devote themselves whole-heartedly to some other useful tasks, especially if those are missional tasks. I have a good friend who retired from Shell Oil in his early fifties. He turned to giving lots more time to mission and ministry tasks and to helping out in his town on the town council and doing good public works. He was hardly idle or "gone fishin'," or "spending his grandchildren's inheritance." He was still a very useful member of society and a good servant of Christ and his church. If this is all one means by "retirement," then by all means retire. But actually this shouldn't be called retirement. It should be called reallocation of time and resources and efforts.

If you have spent any time at all in the antechamber of heaven, by which I mean nursing homes (another entirely modern invention so that families can be shed of the daily burden of taking care of the elderly), you can smell the loneliness, the sense

7. Jürgen Moltmann, *Theology of Play* (New York: Harper & Row, 1972), p. 34.

of abandonment by family, the lack of sense of purpose and meaning anymore, in such places. I am not saying that there are never times or conditions in which someone may need to be institutionalized, or have daily in-home care. There are, of course, such times and conditions. My point is that the Christian should not *normally* work toward retirement or life in retirement homes. I give thanks to God for the great work of the Hospice organization that allows a person to die with dignity at home and not in the sterile environment of the hospital. As Christians we honestly need to rethink the whole issue of healthcare in so many ways. Consider the following.

It is the practice of doctors and hospitals to keep patients alive at all times and at almost all costs. The reason for this is a mantra — "This life is all there is; we must prop it up and keep it going at all costs." The hospitals have become the secular equivalent of sanctuaries, the doctors the high priests, and the credo — making the most of and extending as long as possible life in this mortal frame. But frankly, the Christian does not believe this. He or she does not believe that this life is the be-all and end-all of human existence. And if you don't believe that, then you have to ask questions especially about end-of-life care, like "Is this treatment prolonging the living or prolonging the dying?" Christians who believe in everlasting life can sit more lightly with such questions because they do not believe the answers to such questions are a matter of eternal life and eternal death. Surgery questions, ventilator questions, morphine questions are never ultimate questions for Christians, as this life is just stage one of human existence. And so, we must rethink the whole way we approach life, health, rest, sleep, etc. in light of the Kingdom that will come. Why endlessly try to prop up this decaying flesh, when a resurrection body is in the offing? That's the sort of question one needs to ask as a Christian.

But it's not just retirement questions and end-of-life questions that should come in for close scrutiny in light of the Kingdom. There is also the issue of sabbaticals for folk like me — teachers. In one sense the term *sabbatical* is euphemistic — schools grant teachers time off every so often *if they have a valid or vital writing project or ministry project that might justify the so-called "time off."* It isn't actually time off. It is simply time more singularly focused on some specific ministry or writing tasks. That's all. It hardly deserves to be called a sabbatical. There is no ceasing from work involved! You just become more task specific. Even worse, schools that grant sabbaticals usually do so with strings attached — you promise to serve the school for an additional two years or so. Not much of a "sabbatical" in the biblical sense.

I do, however, think that the year of Jubilee provisions for persons and lands should be rethought by Christians in light of the Kingdom. I suggest this because Jesus himself intimates in his inaugural sermon in Luke 4 that he is bringing in the year of Jubilee, which includes debt release, prisoner release, slaves manumitted, land allowed to lie fallow, and the like. If Jesus' bringing in of the Kingdom signals the eschatological Jubilee period, then we have been in that period for a long time now, and it should have affected the way we view all the things discussed in this chapter — Sabbath, rest, sleep, retirement, sabbaticals, all these related subjects. And when all those subjects are reconfigured in light of the Kingdom, this also means that work as well has to be reconfigured and rethought, as I have argued at length in the book *Work*. Work and rest are reciprocals, and what one says about a Kingdom view of the former affects what one can and should say about a Kingdom perspective on the latter.

Jesus the vision-caster said he came to set the prisoners free, to heal the sick, to preach good news to the poor (hence debt forgiveness in the Lord's prayer). The Kingdom is supposed to be all about healing, helping, restoring, emancipating, and you will notice that all those activities happen during the "sabbatical" year! As it turns out, the Kingdom is not just about rest, it's about restoration; it's not just about restoration, it's also about restitution. We live now in the light of Jesus' proclaimed Jubilee. The question for us becomes: What have we done to implement it — not merely to find rest, but to give it, not merely to experience restoration but to share, not merely to obtain forgiveness, but to grant it, not merely to know wholeness and holiness, but to share it? Are we, like Christ, wounded healers, or have we just laid down our burdens for our own personal and private rest and sleep? I want to leave you with a story of Jubilee.

Some years after the end of apartheid in South Africa, I went and gave lectures at four of the major universities there. I was particularly struck by the people I met, especially in Pretoria in the theology department, and by my visit with Bishop Peter Storey in Stellenbosch. In the first instance I met a black South African scholar who had paid the full price for his resistance to apartheid. He had not merely been incarcerated like Mandela, he had been tortured. And yet, here he was working in a theology department with various Afrikaners. Just the very act of his doing so proclaimed forgiveness and Jubilee, and a rest to all the hostilities. My theory is that unless there is a sabbatical, by which I mean a ceasing from hostilities, real Jubilee is not possible.

Peter Storey told me all about the Truth and Reconciliation Commissions. It is a remarkable, and remarkably Christian thing that happened — quite different from the Nuremberg trials, for example. In those commissions the Afrikaners who tormented black men and women were given the chance to come forward and openly confess their sins, and be forgiven without further reprisals. They were to apologize to those present whom they had harmed, personally and directly. I have watched a film of some of those confessions and tearful acts of forgiveness. The Kingdom was coming with observation in those days, and it made possible the going forward of a nation of blacks and whites that needed to overcome the racial hatred and prejudices that had scarred the past. It is a truly remarkable story, and you get a small glimpse of it in the stirring recent film — *Invictus.*

When the Kingdom comes in a life, in a city, in a nation, it brings healing in its wings; it brings rest, and restoration, and even sleep without fear of danger. It brings Jubilee. But there are many more dimensions to the Kingdom perspective, and in our next chapter we will turn to the matter of play — a theology of play, in the light of the Kingdom. As we shall see, even the ordinary Christian life can be extraordinary if it is lived to the glory of God, for the edification of others, and on the basis of the coming Kingdom and its values.

In Sum

Christians are not called to, nor required to, follow the retrospective approach of sabbatarianism when it comes to the issue of rest and sleep and restoration. We live out of the new creation and Kingdom that is coming, not out of the old creation and form of this world that is passing away. We are no longer under the Mosaic provisions; rather we are new covenant people looking forward to the Day of the Lord, and celebrating the first Lord's Day, the Day of resurrection. We live betwixt and between, as the Kingdom has already come and is yet to come. How this affects our theology of rest and restoration is that we still need rest and restoration, but this does not require keeping Sabbath. What it requires is rest and restoration every single day, and it requires a good balance in the normal Christian life between work and rest, and play, and a myriad of other activities.

We have made pertinent Christian distinctions not only between Sabbath and rest, but also between rest and sleep. God neither slumbers nor sleeps, but we do. God, however, has a rest, and the author of Hebrews calls us to enter that eschatological rest of God — not as a resting place or resting time, but as a state of being, living by faith, with the peace of Christ in our hearts, looking forward without anxiety about the future, because the future is as bright as God's promises and dawning Kingdom.

Worship as defined by Jesus is not about sacred space or times or days but about worship in spirit and truth, whenever and wherever; for every day, in the proper sense, is the Lord's day, and the wall of partition between the sacred and secular has been broken down by the death and resurrection of Jesus. All of life is to be hallowed, all of our activities should be doxological — done to the glory of God and for the edification of others. This means as well that our resting time is also sacred time. It is something God gives his loved ones — who need their rest.

Rest, like sleep, is a gift, not a right, just as life is a gift, not a right. There is a relief in resting, and we rest by faith. When we lie down to sleep, we lie down trusting the Lord will look after us at our most vulnerable; we lay down our burdens and give up the control of our lives. And thus sleep becomes a metaphor for trusting God, for "letting go and letting God." It is not merely a gift from God, but as we submit to it, we offer ourselves back to God again, saying our evening prayers.

In rest, as in shalom, we experience the presence and peace of God, who even speaks to us at times in our dreams. Like waking shalom, this peace from rest and sleep makes us whole. It not merely restores us so we can go back to our daily activities, it reminds us day after day — "Remember your mortal frame, your weakness, your vulnerability, your creaturely needs. Remember you are not God in your life, nor Lord over your life." When this is realized we can hear the word of the Lord given to Paul — "My power is made perfect in your weakness, my grace is sufficient for you." When the Day of eschatological Jubilee arrives, so will justice and righteousness and peace and love and emancipation and freedom, and restoration. The dreams of all the prophets will be realized, and all the plans of God for his people will come to fruition.

At the end of all things, in the new creation, we will look forward to the consummation of the Lord's Day, as we fully become Easter people, with resurrection bodies like that of Christ. As there will be no more night, we may wonder if, as well, we will need no more sleep. More certainly, there will be no temple in the new creation, no celebration of old creation rules, no division between sacred and secular, for the presence of the Lord will suffuse all of his creation, and joy will be our abiding companion. Just as there is something greater than faith and hope and more enduring — namely love, there is also something greater than rest and sleep and peace, namely joy. In our next chapter we must talk about a foretaste of that joy. We must discuss play.

CHAPTER TWO

Play On

I wonder whether it is possible . . . to regain the idea of the Church as providing an understanding of the area of freedom (art, education, friendship, play . . .). Who is there . . . in our times who can devote himself with an easy mind to music, friendship, games, or happiness? Surely not "the ethical man," but only the Christian.

Dietrich Bonhoeffer, *Letters and Papers from Prison,*
January 23, 1944

Taking Play Seriously

The normal Christian life has many different facets and features. It involves many different activities. And if that life is healthy and wants to be happy, it certainly involves more than a modicum of play. Instinctively, children know this. We structure playtime into their schedules, even into their school schedules. Too many adults for some reason sometimes think it is childish if they also engage in play. More's the pity.

It will be well to keep steadily in mind throughout the reading of this chapter that play is not the same thing as rest — *at all.*

Time off from work for rest and sleep is very different than time off from work for play, and both are needed. When Christians lose their ability to play, their desire to play, their interest in playing, they are moving away from, rather than toward, "turning and becoming as a child" so they may inherit the kingdom of God. In other words, from a Christian point of view, turning away from play as if it were frivolous, as if it were something adults should leave behind, is itself a sign of immaturity and reflects a lack of Christian wisdom. It's like saying "I'm an adult now and I only have time for serious things, not for things that could be characterized as just fun."

But suppose I put it this way: Is it really a mature move to turn your back on good things that can bring you joy, that can improve your mental agility, that can improve your physical fitness, that can give you social skills and help you learn how to be a team player? I think not. Indeed, I would say that work and worship both have something to learn from play. For example, I have often wished that the enthusiasm and joy and celebration I sometimes see at games would also be what I see in worship.

We began a discussion of play in my book on the Kingdom perspective on work, and it will be well if we refresh our memories about a few things that were said there.[1] Play can be seen as an eschatological activity as well as a childlike one. Jürgen Moltmann, for example, stresses that in playing we anticipate our liberation, a time when we study war no more, a time when we shed all those things that inhibit us and alienate us from real life. Play foreshadows the joy of the eschaton where all manner of drudgery and disease and decay and death will be left behind.[2] Play is quite rightly seen as a celebration of life lived to its fullest, its fastest, its highest, its limits. And play is something that has some potential to unite

1. Witherington, *Work: A Kingdom Perspective on Labor* (Grand Rapids: Eerdmans, 2011), pp. 145-54.

2. Jürgen Moltmann, *A Theology of Play* (New York: Harper & Row, 1972), p. 3.

The Rest of Life

us, if done well and wisely. The Olympic vision and spirit of its games reflect this to a small degree. In any case, I think Moltmann is right that games, played well and fairly, fuel a theology of hope for the future. Playing is not a useless activity. It anticipates the joy of the eschaton.

In light of our last chapter we need to say something about rest and its relationship to play. Play is not a form of work (unless you are a professional athlete of some sort). Nor is play the antithesis of work. Indeed it may be much more strenuous than work. Playing then is not a form of resting either; it is an entity in itself. Some people see playing as a waste of time. I entirely disagree. Just because something is neither rest nor work nor worship doesn't make it a waste of time. Just because something is not part of your vocation or calling doesn't make it a waste of time. Indeed, just because you are playing a game that you are not necessarily very adept at does not make it a waste of time.

Games are exercises in ethics. Let me illustrate this point by talking about a game I still play regularly. Few games are more ethical in their obvious myriad rules than golf. Golf is Old Testamental about rules, but you have to call penalties on yourself. It's largely a self-policing sport, even in professional tournaments. This makes it rather different from, say, baseball with its umpires, or basketball and football with their referees. Indeed, in a game like baseball the home-plate umpire sometimes has more say in the outcome of a game than the players, if it is a low-scoring or close game that depends on called balls and strikes for the outcome.

Games in a sense mirror life. There are rules, but whether you abide by them or not is another matter. In football and basketball there is an awful lot of violating of rules on almost every play. Whether we think of a holding call in football or a foul call in basketball, these could be multiplied infinitely and the games would grind to a halt. This is far less of a problem in golf or chess or even baseball. My point is this — *games are morality plays in miniature, and we find out what kind of person a person is by how they play.* Do they play fair? Do they cheat?

I have loved baseball since I was a child, and very few people have been more disappointed by the steroid era than a fan like me. This sort of cheating destroys the integrity of the game in various ways, not least in that an unfair advantage is gained. But games are not *just* morality plays that reveal the character of the players. They also reveal the character of the fans or spectators. Most of us have had the uncomfortable experience of watching fans, especially those who have been drinking too much, who are so biased that they think every call that goes against their team must be wrong, and they boo and shout epithets. This is hardly good sportsmanship; it's just partisanship. If play at its worst is prospective in that it mirrors hell (a hell where cheaters prosper, and the rich only get richer), play at its best is also prospective — of the Kingdom.

Consider the following true story. In April 2008, two college softball teams were playing their second game in a conference doubleheader. In the second inning, Western Oregon senior Sara Tucholsky hit the first home run of her career over the center field fence. Though exciting for Tucholsky and her team, the really noteworthy part of the story was what happened next.

As Tucholsky began to round the bases, she didn't quite tag first base and went back to tag it. As she reversed direction, her knee suddenly gave out, leaving her crumpled on the field in great pain, a few feet from the base. She was completely unable to continue rounding the bases under her own power.

The umpires confirmed that the only option available under the rules was to replace Tucholsky at first base with a pinch runner. The hit would then be recorded as a two-run single instead of a three-run home run. If Tucholsky received any assistance from coaches or trainers while she was an active runner, she would be out. The coach had no choice but to prepare to make the substitution, which would take Tucholsky's only home run away from her.

At that point, Central Washington senior Mallory Holtman stepped forward and asked if it would be okay if her team carried Tucholsky around the bases and helped her tag each one. Even though the outcome of the game — Holtman's final game at home — would decide her own opportunity for a first postseason appearance, she stepped up to help a player she knew only as an opponent for four years.

"Honestly, it's one of those things that I hope anyone would do for me," Holtman said. "She hit the ball over the fence. She's a senior; it's her last year. . . . I think anyone who knew that we could touch her would have offered to do it, just because it's the right thing to do. She was obviously in agony."

So, while the fans gave them a standing ovation, Holtman and shortstop Liz Wallace carried Tucholsky slowly around the bases, in what reporter Graham Hays calls perhaps "the longest and most crowded home run trot in the game's history."

In the end, Western Oregon won the game. But what will be remembered about this game is not who won or lost. As Western Oregon's coach said, "It kept everything in perspective. . . . It was such a lesson that we learned — that it's not all about winning. And we forget that, because as coaches, we're always trying to get to the top. We forget that. But I will never, ever forget this moment. It's changed me, and I'm sure it's changed my players."[3]

There are so many positive things to say about this story. What this story suggests is that playing according to the rules, and fairly, is what it is all about. It's not mainly about winning and losing. I'm afraid that much of what passes for sports in America has completely forgotten the meaning of *play* and of sportsmanship. Of course people want to win, but even when it comes to playing, there are things more important than winning. The old dictum "It's not whether you win or lose, it's how you play the game" is a good one,

3. As reported by ESPN writer Graham Hays. This story accessed on the ESPN website June 6, 2011, but the story ran on April 28, 2008.

but frankly it is not the motto of many players or teams these days. But it was the motto of Mallory Holtman in the story recounted above. Even in play, sometimes just finishing requires considerable help, even help from opponents, and it is worth the whole effort.

The story also has the eschatological element of *last chance*. I remember what that feels like. I was in my last year of playing basketball, and my team was in the championship game. I scored the first eight points of the game. But the coach's son also played my position, and he played the remaining three quarters. We lost the championship. I was only a teenager and had no say in the matter, but I felt the sense of personal loss because I would never have a chance to do that again, and I was sure I could have made a difference. I think I understand entirely the feelings and attitude of Mallory Holtman in the story above. There would be no more chances for Sara Tucholsky. It was now or never. So Sara was given an assist from an unlikely source — the opposition. This is a story of self-sacrifice, and play can often depict for us the kinds of stories that in fact have gospel character.

Play also gives us a chance to reveal courage. I was fortunate enough to run in the 1993 Boston Marathon. It was a very hot day, that Patriot's Day, which is odd for early April in Boston. But almost from the start of the race there was something epiphanic and revelatory about running in that race.

Before the race began, I knew with certainty it was never about winning *for me*. I had no chance of winning. I only hoped to finish as a forty-two-year-old man. I went to the front of the pack before the gun sounded just to look at the elite runners — mostly Africans with huge thighs and otherwise unnaturally little muscle mass in the upper torsos and arms. I had no ambition, hope, or possibility of winning the Boston Marathon that day. I finished ahead of many, including the mayor, and behind hundreds and hundreds of elite runners. Winning was out of the question. As St. Paul says, however, it was about running a good race, an honest race, a straight race, and finishing the course.

What impressed me far more than seeing the elite runners was watching a man I ran alongside of for quite a good period of time — he was running while pushing his quadriplegic son in a wheelchair the entire race course to the finish line. Now that was a profile in courage! You could see the joy on the face of the young man in the chair, and the tears coming down the face of the running father. That alone was worth the price I paid to run and finish that whole race.

Running, something I have done for most of my life, is indeed rather like life and it's also like faith — you fight the good fight, you run the full race, and you finish — you finish the course. When I finished the Boston Marathon my friend Rick who lives in Boston was waiting for me at the finish line and took my picture. They wrapped me in NASA foil, gave me fluids, and I collapsed in a heap. But it was a good heap — a heap of accomplishment for me anyway.

Many of the elite runners had gone out too fast, much too fast, and with too little water. I passed many of them at the halfway point. They were on stretchers on the side of the road getting IVs near Wellesley. It was so hot that Alberto Salazar, who had won the New York Marathon, dropped out at Heartbreak Hill. I ran up that hill with a seventy-something-year-old grandmother exhorting me — "Let's run up this hill!" It's a good lesson in humility to be shamed into picking up the pace on Heartbreak Hill by a grandmother.

Along the twenty-six-mile course, when you run a good race there are surprises. When I got to Newton, the boys at the Newton Fire Department hosed me down, and then wanted a picture with me. Why? Not because I was such a spiffy elite runner, but because I bore the number 1993, which was the year of the race. So I took a brief time out for a photo. I wish I had that photo. Along the race of life, you get Kodak moments and help at unexpected times and in unexpected places. And when you play, there are a lot more of those kinds of memorable moments.

Towards the end of the marathon when I was really grinding it out, I was heading toward the Prudential Center near the finish line, and the Boston College students on the Green Line subway (it comes above ground at that point) rolled down the windows on the train and cheered me on. I kept saying, "Are you running with me, Jesus, are you running with me?" I was out of gas. There weren't even fumes left. But there was determination to finish, even if I had to crawl across the line. And here's an interesting insight on how play can fuel other aspects of the normal Christian life.

What I needed after this sort of strenuous "play" was a hot bath and then rest, sleep. . . . Lots of it. Had I actually accomplished anything? Yes I had. I had learned a lot about my own character and stamina. But playing is not just about finding and testing your limits or even just improving your endurance and perseverance. It's also about the imitation of the divine.

One of the most interesting of Moltmann's points about play is that it shares something in common with God's creation. Since God is a self-sufficient being, creating the universe was not necessary. Similarly play, in absolute terms, is not a *necessity* of life. It is not necessary in the same way that rest or eating or sleeping or working is necessary. One can *exist* without play. But human beings were not made to merely exist. They were made in God's image to worship God and to emulate his actions, and in "play" we do emulate God's actions. We create a game and play a game that has a universe of its own, its own rules, its own gravitational pull so to speak. It is a little world unto itself. If we ask the cosmic question — Why is there something instead of nothing? one answer is — Because God is playful. God enjoys creating and playing. But there is more.

Like the creation, man's games are an expression of freedom, not caprice, for playing relates to the joy of the Creator with his creation and the pleasure of the player with his game. Like creation, games combine sincerity and mirth, suspense and relaxation. The player is wholly absorbed in his game and takes it seriously, yet at the same time he transcends himself and his game, for it is after all a game. So he is realizing his freedom without losing it. He steps outside of himself without selling himself. The symbol of the world as God's free creation out of his good pleasure corresponds to the symbol of man as the child of God.[4]

If you don't think God is playful, you haven't examined his creation much lately. What kind of God makes a duck-billed platypus or a funny old bird like an ostrich or for that matter a giraffe? When you actually start examining creation closely, if it doesn't make you smile and then laugh, then you have no sense of humor. God certainly has a sense of humor and a sense of play. Or consider the fact that children have all this endless energy, and hardly need it. You don't need endless energy to play in a sandbox. Adults need the energy all the time, and often find themselves lacking it. What's up with that?

But play is not just fun and something to make us laugh. It is not just a holy distraction from the disasters of life. It is not, as Moltmann reminds us, just an opiate for the oppressed masses, though it has often been used that way by ruthless dictators. Think, for example, of the 1936 Olympic Games in Hitler's Germany, and the heroic running of Jesse Owens, who absolutely falsified the Nazi propaganda about the master race and the inferior other races. Play cannot merely show us the humor of God; it can reveal the justice and fairness of God as well. One of the most frequent remarks I heard from Red Sox fans after they finally won the World Series in 2004 was — "There is a God!" By this was meant: justice and fairness have finally been served.

But there is a different kind of play we will also need to talk

4. Moltmann, *A Theology of Play*, p. 18.

about in this chapter. I mean the Play, and plays, and playwrights, and playing music, and dancing. Consider music. Music can minister to persons in parts of their soul that mere talking doesn't reach. Many films would fall flat if they didn't have music to heighten the tension, presage what is coming, and move the affective side of audience members to embrace the story or hero. Music functions much the same way in worship. Its function in worship is not (1) to entertain the audience, nor (2) to rev up the troops, nor (3) to provide an interlude between tedious or turgid discourses. Its function is to help us all be caught up in love and wonder and praise of God, so that our whole selves are worshiping. Whether it's through music or the visual arts or dance or drama, worship requires these forms of playing.

We have all seen graceful athletes in motion, and so there is an aesthetic to that sort of play, but there is even more obviously an aesthetic dimension to the so-called fine arts. Music, for example, is supposed to move us in ways that make us reflect on the nature of beauty and harmony and the like. Having been involved in music all my life, I can attest to how very essential this kind of play — playing music, whether actively (I sing, play string instruments and piano) or passively (by intently listening). These preliminary observations are simply meant to tease our minds into active thought and confront us with the fact that play is important. It is not frivolous or pointless — and theological reflection on play is thus essential if we are going to have a meaningful theology of the normal Christian life. "Play relativizes our 'over-seriousness' toward life, filling us with a spirit of joy and delight that carries over into all aspects of our existence. This attitude is based in and fosters the tacit recognition of a restored humanity that senses its rootedness in life's fundamental sacredness."[5] Bearing these things in mind, we can now turn to a definition of play.

5. R. K. Johnston, *The Christian at Play* (Eugene, OR: Wipf & Stock, 1997), pp. 48-49.

Defining Play

It will perhaps not surprise you to learn that there is a dearth of meaningful theological studies of play. Indeed, as I searched far and wide, after Moltmann's tiny little volume from the early '70s, there has been almost nothing but the sound of silence on this topic, which is amazing considering how sports- and music-crazy the world is. Fortunately, there was one detailed doctoral dissertation done on the subject by Robert K. Johnston, who studied under one of my mentors, Thomas Langford, at Duke University in the mid-'70s. Johnston revised and expanded it into a book (*The Christian at Play*, 1982) that was then printed and reprinted as late as 1997, and then again by another publisher more recently. When you see a little book have this sort of life long after it is first published, you realize two things: (1) it was a valuable study, and (2) no one or almost no one thereafter picked up the ball on this important topic and ran with it further. In this chapter we intend to interact with Johnston and hopefully make a little more progress down the field. Johnston defines play as follows:

> I would understand play as that activity which is freely and spontaneously entered into, but which, once begun, has its own design, its own rules or order, which must be followed so that play may continue. The player is called into play by a potential co-player and/or play object, and while at play, treats other players and/or play things as personal, creating with them a community that can be characterized by "I-Thou" rather than "I-It" relationships. This play has a new time (playtime) and a new space (a playground) that function as "parentheses" in the life and world of the player. The concerns of the everyday life come to a temporary standstill in the mind of the player, and the boundaries of his or her world are redefined. Play, to be play, must be entered into without outside purpose: it cannot be connected with a material interest or ulterior motive, for

then the boundaries of the playground and the limits of the playtime are violated. But though play is an end in itself, it can nevertheless have several consequences. Chief among these are the joy and release, the personal fulfillment, the remembering of our common humanity, and the presentiment of the sacred, which the player sometimes experiences in and through the activity. One's participation in the adventure of playing, even given the risk of injury or defeat, finds resolution at the end of the experience, and one re-enters ongoing life in a new spirit of thanksgiving and celebration. The player is a changed individual because of the playtime, his or her life having been enlarged beyond the workaday world.[6]

I think these observations are all helpful, though I do wonder what professional athletes, whose play is their work and vice versa, would say about all this. Play is not time out for them; it is time to go to work. And one wonders how much this stifles the joy or domesticates or even eliminates one of the very things play was meant to accomplish — namely time out from work. Professional athletes enter into play clearly enough with a material interest and an outside purpose. This is why some would say professional players, oddly enough, like professional playwrights, are not playing. Play, in the minds of observers like Johnston, is an activity that is outside the context of work, and done for the pleasure it brings, not for some utilitarian or pragmatic purpose. This is also why, for example, "exercising" is not the same thing as playing. Exercising in the first place is not a sport or at least not a team sport, and it is undertaken for a specific purpose, namely staying or getting into reasonable physical condition. It is not an end in itself; it is a means to an end. But play and playing are an end in themselves.

Johan Huizinga's study of play concludes, "[W]e might call it a free activity standing quite consciously outside 'ordinary' life as

6. Johnston, *The Christian at Play,* p. 34.

being 'not serious,' but at the same time absorbing the player intensely and utterly. It is an activity connected with no material interest, and no profit can be gained by it. It proceeds within its own proper boundaries of time and space according to fixed rules and in an orderly manner. It promotes the formation of social groupings."[7]

On this showing, no players in the NBA, NFL, MLB, etc. are actually playing. They are professional athletes performing a task, which may explain why managers and others begin to complain when their players start "playing around" rather than taking their jobs or tasks on the field of play seriously enough. You can see why such players get frustrated and confused at times. Are they not supposed to be playing, are they not supposed to be spontaneous and enjoy and celebrate what they are doing? Why in the world are there rules against celebrating in the end zone?

The problem is simple — many players assume they are playing, but alas, their owners, managers, handlers, referees, and sometimes even their fans think they are not. No, they are supposed to be working hard so some things can be accomplished — namely winning championships and making money. On both Johnston's and Huizinga's definitions of playing, what these sports heroes are doing is not "play" strictly speaking. And this brings us to why college athletes are not, and should not be, paid to play. Paid athletes cease to have the freedom and creativity of real play. This play becomes something utilitarian; it becomes work. Part of the beauty of college athletics is that it is done for its own merits, its own joys, its own internal or inherent rewards, its own group-building and character-building benefits, not for some fringe benefit or work purpose.

Play is not about punching a clock; indeed one of its major characteristics is that it has its own space and time and rules apart

7. J. Huizinga, *Homo Ludens: A Study of the Play Element in Culture* (Boston: Beacon Press, 1955), p. 7.

from that of the real world, and indeed, in the case of a game like baseball, it is untimed — timeless. Players often remark on the different sense of time when they are playing. Some will say that as they are making a dramatic catch or swinging at a baseball things seem to slow down or go in slow motion, almost stopping, until the act is accomplished.

Play creates its own imaginary world, its own necessary space. For example, suppose there was a city ordinance declaring that keeping valuable objects, for instance baseballs found on a city street, was against the law. This law would not, however, apply within the ballpark itself when a home run was hit and a fan caught it. Or suppose there was a little door in the wall known as the Green Monster at Fenway Park, through which an outfielder could run right through to the street outside of a stadium. Suppose for a minute someone hits a mammoth fly ball that is going over the wall. If the player ran through the door and out onto the street and caught the ball, the batter would not be out, as the player had left his legally bounded space within which the game is played. He can lean over a fence and catch a ball or climb a wall and catch a ball, but he can't run up the stairs in the outfield bleachers and catch a ball. Games have their own ethics, their own morals, their own rules — and yes, indeed, they are morality plays. Cheating, whether it involves corking a bat or something else, is definitely inauthentic play, bogus playing. Leaving the field of play to make a play is definitely not allowed; it's out of bounds, and all sports involve bounded universes. But within the field of play, a baseball fielder can run, jump, slide, improvise, catch the ball with one hand, two hands, barehanded, gloved hands — there is lots of room for freedom and improvisation. I remember watching pitcher Mark Buehrle of the Chicago White Sox at the beginning of the 2010 baseball season make the play of the year. The ball was in play but caroming outside the first base line. Buehrle, huffing and puffing, raced over, picked up the ball, but was facing in entirely the wrong direction to throw it to the first

The Rest of Life

baseman. What did he do? He scooped up the ball and chucked it blindly through his legs to the first baseman, making the play. He improvised. Yes, there is freedom and excitement within the bounded field of dreams.[8]

What is missing, however, in the definitions of play cited above is the eschatological or kingdom dimension of play. By this I mean that play foreshadows a time when we have not only set aside all our hostilities and our necessity of "making a living" but when we as community can enjoy doing things together that involve the celebration of life, and are not matters of life and death, are not life threatening, and reflect a time of harmony and cooperation and communion and team spirit and koinonia. Play is time out from work, but it is not rest time either. It is Kingdom foreshadowing. Let me illustrate.

On my last trip to New Orleans, for a conference at New Orleans Baptist Seminary, we took time out from all our lecturing, preaching, and debating to enjoy a good meal in the French Quarter and then go to a jazz club. Now, as it happened, we were there during the pre–Mardi Gras season. If any town knows how to party and play, it is New Orleans. They hardly need an invitation or excuse to start marching, singing, dancing, playing; you get the picture. The saints go marching in with regularity there, and they don't even have to wait for Fat Tuesday or for a funeral or for the New Orleans Saints to finally win a Super Bowl (which they did, and some thought it was a clear sign of the end times being at hand; surely something eschatological was happening).

Anyway, we went to Snug Harbor, a tiny little jazz club where Ellis Marsalis and members of his family play regularly on Friday nights. Ellis is the father of a whole brood of musicians, including Wynton and Branford, to mention but two. What struck me, how-

8. Johnston, *The Christian at Play*, p. 44, suggests that a professional ball player could still be said to be playing if he was not doing it for the money and fame, but simply for the "love of the game." I suppose there must be some pros like that, but I have seldom encountered them.

ever, is that out on all the streets around this club people were celebrating, partying, playing their musical instruments, singing, and having a great time. Just to get into the club, we had to plow through various joyful and fun-loving people, young and old, who did not need to pay money to go into a club or into a stadium but could just play and celebrate right there in the street. They were not engaged in "pay to play"; they were just caught up in *joie de vivre* and were playing right there in the streets spontaneously without permission or invitation, and it was so infectious that lots of bystanders were joining in the dancing and singing.

Now I imagine there will be lots of scenes like that in the Kingdom. Okay, maybe there will be less inebriation, but certainly no less being caught up in love, and wonder, and joy. These folks had lost themselves in the moment, forgotten about their sorrows, and were having a good time. But here's the thing — this was not merely an escape *from* reality. *It was a momentary escape into the future reality that God intended for us all.*

Consider for a moment a text that describes the year of the Lord's favor, the year of Jubilee (a text that Jesus began to recite in Nazareth at his inaugural sermon announcing the Kingdom). The Servant says:

> The Spirit of the Lord is upon me, because the Lord has anointed me to . . . comfort all who mourn, and to provide for those who grieve in Zion — to bestow on them a crown of beauty instead of ashes, the oil of joy instead of mourning, and a garment of praise instead of a spirit of despair. They will be called mighty oaks, a planting of the Lord for the display of his splendor. (Isa. 61:1-3)

Only a moment's reflection is required to see the relevance of such a text to the revelers on that night in New Orleans. Hurricane Katrina devastated that city. Waterside Baptist Church, a church where I have preached, came to be called Under Water Baptist.

Thousands of homes and businesses were destroyed, many lives were lost, and many thought New Orleans could never recover. And in truth, it is still in the process of recovery. But one of the things that has most helped them carry on with the hard work of recovery and to rejoice instead of just mourn was *play* and the spirit of hope for the future that comes through play. If the Ain'ts can become the Saints and win a Super Bowl, then much is possible. Play foreshadows an eschatological better day when things go right, and this is worth celebrating now. *The foreshadowing of better times is itself a foretaste of better times, and this is in part the theological function of play.* It is not enough to say that play provides relaxation, elevation of the spirits, escape from reality, or pleasure, but serves no utilitarian purpose.

While play does do those things, play is also teleological. It performs no immediate service or utilitarian purpose, but it points to a future goal, a future state, a future time when the harmony and joy of play become the harmony and joy and play of all life, free from disease, decay, and death, free from suffering, sin, and sorrow. Free to be all we were intended to be. There is a reason play stimulates the imagination and suggests to us, in the words of Kevin Garnett when he and his Celtics finally won a championship, that "anything is possible!"[9] Play was meant to point us forward toward a better day, a better time, a more harmonious world where all manner of things are well. Play suggests to us the full possibilities of what we can be, the hint of what it means to really live, to be fully human, to have real brothers or sisters in arms, all on the same team playing together toward the same end. This goes beyond camaraderie to koinonia.

There are other good by-products of good play. For one thing, a player realizes, if he is wise, that he is blessed — blessed to be able to play when not all can do so. He realizes that it is important not to take all things so seriously. A person without play or a sense

9. See Johnston, *The Christian at Play*, p. 45.

of play tends to take everything far too seriously, and to take losses far too hard. "Play relativizes our over-seriousness toward life filling us with a spirit of joy and delight that carries over into all aspects of our existence."[10] The player also realizes that there are forces larger than himself that have enabled this or that good play. How many players have you heard say, "Fortunately, the wind was blowing in on that day, so when I over hit the ball, it did not fly beyond the green and into the water" or, "Fortunately the outfielder slipped a bit on the wet grass, which slowed down his throwing the ball just barely enough so that I slid in under the catcher's tag." Or on the other end of the spectrum, when a Mr. Bartman reached out over the wall to grab an incoming fly ball, thus preventing Cubs fielder Moise Alou from making the catch, it all came unraveled for the Cubs' playoff hopes after that. And it was one more year of no trip to the World Series, a trend that began at the end of World War I! It is not a surprise that players talk about blessing or providence or something larger than themselves helping to determine the outcome of their playing. Playing not only expresses a person's full limits and full physical potential. It also reminds us all too clearly of what our limits are, of how we need help to play well, and not just help from teammates either.

As ridiculous and clichéed as it sometimes sounds, when a player first thanks God after something truly good has happened to him or to his team, it is because he realizes he is part of something bigger than himself that has meaning and purpose and brings joy to human lives. He is part of something worth celebrating. When my beloved Red Sox finally won the World Series in 2004, millions turned out to see the parade in Boston. You would have thought the Minutemen had won the Revolutionary War all over again! Instead it was just a party celebrating play — playing and winning, yes, but also the quality of play. I will be replaying in my mind until I pass away Dave Roberts stealing second base,

10. Johnston, *The Christian at Play*, p. 48.

leading to the first of four straight victories over the dreaded Yankees in the American League Championship Series, and then on to four quick victories in the World Series. That one little act, that one little play, set an avalanche in motion that could not be stopped until victory had fully come. Any moral thing, even play, that keeps hope alive and gives joy to the oppressed, or forlorn, or lonely, or depressed, or pessimistic, is a good thing. "Play can purify our sensibility, make us open again to the gifts of God's goodness which surround us."[11]

Play's Religious Dimensions

It will come as no surprise to those who have studied the so-called Puritan work ethic that the Puritans had little time for, or indeed little tolerance for, adults playing games. Indeed, some of them barely could endure adults playing non-sacred music, much less attending plays. It may well be a partial residue of this attitude that permeated pre-Revolutionary New England, that play, almost from the beginnings of American history, has been seen as something frivolous, something that wastes time and energy, something that serious adults would hardly spend much time on. The reaction, or better said, overreaction to this dour attitude has been the rise of the leisure mentality, the notion that whatever time off from work one has should be spent not in charitable activities or the like, but in leisure or entertainment activities, however defined. Our growing entertainment and leisure culture, and the booming industry that supports it, has made it difficult for theologians to take seriously the subject of a theology of play. But it was not always thus, and surprisingly enough we have help from perhaps unexpected quarters in exploring play's religious dimensions, as we shall now see.

11. Johnston, *The Christian at Play*, p. 52.

When I speak of play's religious dimension I am not merely talking about its psychological dimensions, which may focus on it as an antidote to boredom or ennui, for example. Nor am I talking about play as therapy that helps a person to be a whole person and overcome whatever psychological traumas or troubles the person has. And I am certainly not talking about play as an exercise in sanctioned narcissism, where it's all about me.[12] Moltmann was on the right track when he suggested that Christians should live now in light of the future, and indeed of the eschatological situation that has already begun. In part we usher in God's future, or at least let the world know it's coming, by living now in joy, spontaneously, unselfishly, freely as if playing.[13] Indeed, if the Christian truly believes that God is and will work all things together for good for those who love him and are called to his purposes, then there is much reason to celebrate, to play, even now, in advance of the fullness of the Kingdom's coming.

Peter Berger, the sociologist of knowledge, has given some reflection to the sacred dimension of play, and he suggests that it points to something outside of itself, and that it also participates in that transcendent thing to which it points. On this showing we should call play not merely a sign of the future, but a symbol of it, participating in advance in that to which it points.[14] He adds that play carries within itself the capacity to bring a person to ecstasy, to a condition where he transcends his self-consciousness and self-focus and is surprised by joy, and becomes self-forgetful for a time. I think he is right about this. In play we step outside the taken-for-granted nature of everyday life and open ourselves up to something more, something other than ourselves and beyond ourselves.

12. Unfortunately, this is where we seem to end up in Sam Keen's analysis of play in *To a Dancing God* (New York: Harper & Row, 1970).

13. Moltmann, *A Theology of Play*, pp. 50-52.

14. P. Berger, *A Rumor of Angels* (Garden City, NY: Doubleday, 1970), pp. 64-70.

C. S. Lewis, in his classic little autobiographical book *Surprised by Joy*,[15] talks a good deal about how joy may find a person, unbidden, and surprise him or her; and once a person has had this close encounter with joy, he or she may well be open to all sorts of encounters with the transcendent. Indeed such an experience can turn a cynic into a believer, as it did in Lewis's case. Joy, as it turns out, is the "bright shadow" of holiness, and thus of an encounter with God, the source of all joy and goodness. Play opens up a person to joy, and so is a sort of divine invitation to dance. In play a particular outcome and the euphoria it brings cannot be manipulated or manufactured. One has to just play the game, and joy and ecstasy can come on its own. The point is that God can use play to open people up, and reach them and commune with them. And this includes meeting them in and through the playing of music, not just the playing of what we call games.

Sometimes it is complained that the Bible says nothing about play; it's too serious a book for that. It depends on what you mean by play. If you mean games of the sort we see in modernity, then it is true that we do not find those mentioned in the Bible, though one of the standing jokes about the Bible is this:

Q. When was the first tennis match?
A. When Joseph served in Pharaoh's court.

But it is right to point out that the Bible has quite a lot to say about music, a different form of play (see the psalter, the songbook of Israel, or Job 21:11-12), and indeed it has some things to say about dance, and indeed even Qoheleth tells us there is a time to dance (Eccles. 3:1-4). We are even commanded to praise the Lord with dancing (Ps. 149:3; cf. Ps. 87:7; 150:4). Singing and dancing were a part of celebrating good things (1 Sam. 18:6-7; cf. Judges 11:34; Exod. 15:20-21), including the presence of God in the midst

15. Which first appeared in 1955 (New York: Harcourt, Brace & World).

of his people (2 Sam. 6:5-23). Making merry before the Lord is affirmed in the Bible. What we can say, then, is that certain forms of play are mentioned in the Bible and affirmed, and when one couples that sort of material with passages about celebrating weddings, feasting, rejoicing at various things that are not work and not rest, it becomes clear that the Bible provides both some evidence and also the ethos and rationale for play.

What we have stressed in this chapter is that having a Kingdom view, an eschatological view of life, doesn't cause one to place less emphasis on play; if anything it causes one to place more emphasis on it, as a way of tuning up for Kingdom come. Then, in prime time, it will be time for dance and play of various sorts; indeed we will have an eternity for such things. The very reason we do not now stop playing even in the face of tragedies like Hurricane Katrina or wars like World War II or death itself is because these things too will pass. But joy comes in the morning; it comes with the return of Christ, and we must prepare now for the big celebration. It was John Donne, the great English cleric and poet, who when facing death said this:

> SINCE I am coming to that Holy room,
>   Where, with Thy choir of saints for evermore,
> I shall be made Thy music; as I come
>   I tune the instrument here at the door,
>   And what I must do then, think here before.
> "Hymn to God, My God, in My Sickness"
> (Stanza One)

Playing now, singing now, dancing now is tuning up and practicing for eternity, for Kingdom come, for becoming God's very music, and in small measure we experience the joy and ecstasy and music of that great communion with the One who is our joy, in advance when we do so.

Just a few final thoughts. While play may not be as necessary as work or rest from a purely utilitarian point of view — namely, we must make a living and support ourselves and our family if we have one, and we need rest to do such work — in some ways play is more necessary than either work or rest. Why? Because it is an activity that is an end in itself, not merely a means to an end, and it generates its own joy just in the playing, whatever the outcome may be. For example, just this morning I was standing on a little hill overlooking a green on the back nine of my golf course. Now there was no danger of my winning anything this morning, but when I hit a nearly perfect fifty-foot chip shot that rolled up next to the hole, and then sunk a putt for a par, it brought me real if momentary joy. There is a joy in doing something well and taking care to try and do it well. Like a life lived well, play when it is done well is indeed its own reward and creates joy. Every Christian needs to venture forth into play so there is at least some time in the week that is not a mere means to some other end. This is because in the Kingdom nothing will be a mere means to an end; rather, we will have arrived at the goal and end of all things where we will enjoy where we are, what we are doing, and indeed enjoy God forever. We will be caught up in love and wonder and praise in the eternal moment. It is thus right to seize and relish those moments of playful joy and joyful play now, as previews of coming attractions.

CHAPTER THREE

Food for Thought

*Nothing would be more tiresome than eating and drinking if
God had not made them a pleasure as well as a necessity.*

Voltaire

.

The Bible has plenty to say about eating and drinking, but when is
the last time you saw a book specifically on that subject? Not only
is it a prevalent topic or issue in the Bible; it's even a subject to
pray about, according to Jesus. Yet, upon reflection, I think I know
the reason we don't much find Christian writing about eating and
drinking — the problem is, many Christians have seriously guilty
consciences (especially Western Christians) about their eating
and drinking habits, and they don't want to be reminded of what
they ought to be doing. Let me give you a case in point or two.

I was asked some years ago to speak at the Southern Baptist
Convention in Greensboro, North Carolina. It was an interesting
experience for a United Methodist like me, and one of the saddest
revelations was the physical condition of literally hundreds of
ministers and their wives that I saw at that convention. When I
stood on the platform and looked out at the audience, what I saw
was a considerable majority of the audience who were overweight,

and over 30 percent of the audience certifiably obese or morbidly obese. This shocked me. I knew Americans, including Christians, had diet and exercise problems, but ministers were supposed to be setting good examples in that realm as well as others. What has gone wrong in my lifetime? Maybe we've been following the advice of Mark Twain instead of Dr. Sanjay Gupta. Twain quipped, "Part of the secret of success in life is to eat what you like and let the food fight it out inside."

Not long ago, Duke Divinity School in conjunction with the North Carolina Conferences of the Methodist Church asked all their ministers to take a wellness survey. What prompted this was growing concern about clergy health and clergy burnout, I imagine, and what the survey studied was a variety of interrelated issues that lead to good health. One of these is one's diet. I suspect that one reason this has proved necessary is that we hear little or no teaching in the church about the ethical issues involved in eating and drinking. Indeed, eating seems to have been "declassified" as an ethical issue among most modern Christians. We may eat to live, or in some cases live to eat, but either way we don't view eating as an ethical issue — it's viewed as a matter of necessity, or pleasure, or comfort, but not as a moral issue.

A moment's reflection will show that there is something seriously wrong with this viewpoint. Isn't the Christian's body supposed to be a temple of the Holy Spirit, a place where God takes up residence? Do we really think God wants to live in a landfill? Do we really think it is a good witness to others to abuse our bodies with too much food and the wrong sorts of foods as well? Do we really think it is good stewardship of the gift of life to eat and drink in ways that seriously compromise or threaten our abilities to live that life to the glory of God? I don't think so. But what about all the passages in the Bible about feasting, even eschatological feasting at the Messianic banquet? Doesn't that provide a rationale for overindulging once in a while? What is a correct theological and ethical perspective on food and eating and drinking?

To begin, let's talk about the context in which feasting is discussed in the Bible.

Feasting

There was a famous difference between John the Baptizer and Jesus: one was mainly a faster, subsisting on bugs and wild honey; the other seems to have done a lot of feasting. Jesus kept saying that you shouldn't be mourning and fasting while the bridegroom is with you. There is something about the coming of the Kingdom, like the coming of a wedding, that says, "Let's eat like a King, or in this case, *with* the King." Feasting, in certain contexts, is not only appropriate according to the Bible; it's sanctioned by Jesus himself, as was hospitality in general. We forget, however, that such feasting was for special occasions. It was not every day the father killed the fatted calf; it was only when his prodigal son came home.

Feasting, in the biblical world, if we are talking about ordinary people, was only done at festivals, or on special occasions like weddings. It was not an everyday affair. Indeed, for most of the ancients, the only time they ate meat at all was as part of a meal that resulted from offering a sacrifice to some god. Everyday life involved a much more Spartan diet — bread, wine, olives, dates, fruit; you get the picture. The average diet of the average ancient was nothing like the modern American diet. No wonder Jesus counseled his disciples to pray "Give us this day our daily bread." He did not counsel "Give us this day our daily Big Mac, or hot fudge sundae, or meat-lover's pizza, etc." And in fact, he would not have counseled that if he could have done so. His disciples needed to be able to walk with him twenty miles a day, not waddle one or two on a treadmill.

The social context in which the Bible was written was a context in which people ate just to stay alive. It was all about subsistence, not "the joy of cooking." The only persons who could afford meat or fancy meals with regularity were royalty or the uber-wealthy. The only exception to this was special occasions, festivals, weddings. We do not live in that world. For most of us, every day could be an occasion for a feast, but it shouldn't be. It is only in our age that ordinary persons have to combat obesity, bulimia, anorexia, and the like. There is an old English proverb that says, "He that eats till he is sick must fast till he is well." At least the ancients who attended feasts had the sense to spit much of it out instead of swallowing all of it, however gauche that might appear to us.

In short, what the Bible says about feasting is not encouragement for a modern person to become an aesthete or a grossly overweight individual. It presumes a special occasion, a Kingdom occasion — a wedding, festival, or the like. Getting out of bed is not a special occasion. The truth is, many moderns are simply ruled by their appetites — for food, for sex, for fun — and Christians all too often fall into one or more of these traps. If you are going to have a Kingdom perspective on eating, then feasting needs to be reserved for special occasions, very special occasions. It will be useful just to list the few occasions where feasting is mentioned in the New Testament.

> Matthew 11:19: "The Son of man has come feasting, and they say, See, a lover of food and wine, a friend of tax-farmers and sinners! And wisdom is judged to be right by her works."
>
> Matthew 24:38: "Because as in those days before the overflowing of the waters, they were feasting and taking wives and getting married, till the day when Noah went into the ark."
>
> Luke 7:34: "The Son of man came feasting, and you say, Here is a lover of food and wine, a friend of tax-farmers and sinners."
>
> Luke 12:45: "But if that servant says to himself, My lord is a long time coming; and goes about beating the men-

servants and the women-servants, feasting and taking too much wine . . ."

Luke 17:27: "They were feasting and taking wives and getting married, till the day of the overflowing of the waters, when Noah went into the ark, and they all came to destruction."

Luke 17:28: "In the same way, in the days of Lot; they were feasting and trading, they were planting and building."

1 Corinthians 10:7: "Then do not go after false gods, as some of them did; as it is said in the holy writings, after resting and feasting, the people got up to take their pleasure."

Galatians 5:21: "hard drinking, riotous feasting, and the like. And as to these I forewarn you, as I have already forewarned you, that those who are guilty of such things will have no share in the kingdom of God."

1 Peter 4:3: "Because for long enough, in times past, you have been living after the way of the Gentiles, given up to the desires of the flesh, to drinking and feasting and loose behavior and unclean worship of images."

Jude v. 12: "These are spots in your love-feasts, feasting together with you without fear, pasturing themselves; clouds without water, carried along by the winds; autumnal trees, without fruit, twice dead, rooted up."

What is interesting about this list is that feasting is often associated with immoral behavior, but it is also a regular critique of Jesus' own behavior. Feasting is associated with immoral pagan behavior in particular. The warning in Galatians 5:21 is of particular interest, as it suggests that overindulging in eating and drinking can indeed keep one out of the eschatological Kingdom when it comes on earth! Jude verse 12 is interesting as well, as it suggests that Christians continued to feast, and there is no criticism of their doing so. These meals are called love feasts and were apparently synonymous with Christian meals in homes for the church members in the midst of which the Lord's Supper was consumed (1 Corinthians 11) and there would be teaching. The warning is about allowing false teachers into that sort of intimate setting where the speaker would naturally be trusted and influential. The reason for the association of orgies with feasts and idolatry is that dining in the pagan world often took place at "idol feasts," that is, at feasts in the context of a pagan temple where the god's statue was present at the dinner, and it was assumed the god or goddess was as well. At these feasts, when men got inebriated, there was sexual dalliance with serving girls and others. So idolatry, sexual immorality, and feasting were often associated in such contexts.[1]

It is worth noting as well in these quotes the associating of feasting with the careless living of the immoral, who are caught with forks in their mouths, so to speak, when destruction comes in the time of Noah, and presumably when final judgment comes as well. In any case, there can be no question but that there is an implicit critique of overindulging with any sort of regularity. Indeed, the Galatians verse suggests that such behavior can keep you out of the Kingdom altogether! And here is a good place to tell the stories of the Galloping Gourmet and the Frugal Gourmet. First the latter. Here is his online obituary:

> Jeff Smith, the United Methodist minister who shot to stardom in the 1980s as the "The Frugal Gourmet," died on July 7 of natural causes. He was 65. The Tacoma, Washington, native earned a bachelor's degree from the University of Puget Sound and a master's degree from Drew University. Ordained as a minister in 1965, Smith spent the next six years as a chaplain at the University of Puget Sound, where he taught a course called "Food as Sacrament and Celebration." From 1972 to 1983, Smith

1. On this see Witherington, *Conflict and Community in Corinth: A Socio-Rhetorical Commentary on 1 and 2 Corinthians* (Grand Rapids: Eerdmans, 1996).

owned and operated the Chaplain's Pantry Restaurant and Gourmet Shop, an establishment that also served as a catering service and cooking school. His teaching skills, kind demeanor, and culinary acumen were so renowned that the local PBS affiliate, KTPS-TV, offered him his first show, "Cooking Fish Creatively." It was later renamed "The Frugal Gourmet." Smith moved the show's production to Chicago in the early 1980s, then made a promotional appearance on "The Phil Donahue Show" that garnered more than 45,000 orders for his cookbook. Soon "The Frugal Gourmet" was the most-watched cooking show in the United States, drawing up to 15 million viewers on 300 stations. His 12 cookbooks sold millions of copies and became best-sellers in that genre. He ended every show with his trademark sign-off: "I bid you peace."

There were, sadly, accusations that Smith was guilty of sexual abuse with some men, well before he died, and in fact this caused the cancellation of his show. The allegations were never proved, and indeed the matter was settled out of court. What can be said about Smith, however, is that he wanted to offer something of an alternative to the sort of cooking that only the wealthy and the aesthetes could do — a show like that of Graham Kerr, the famous "Galloping Gourmet." Here is a part of the Wikipedia article about him:

> Graham Kerr (b. 1934) regards himself as a Scot, but grew up in England where his parents were established hoteliers. As a result, much of his childhood was spent among some of the most outstanding chefs of Europe. Educated at the independent school Brighton College, he became trainee manager at the Roebuck Hotel in East Sussex, England, when he was just fifteen years old. After five years in the British Army as catering adviser, Graham became General Manager of England's Royal Ascot Hotel.

Kerr moved to New Zealand in 1958, becoming chief chef catering adviser for the Royal New Zealand Air Force. It was there that his media career began in the early 1960s: his recipes were delivered on radio and in magazines, and a related book, *Entertaining with Kerr,* sold out its first edition in eight days. He moved into television with the emergence of the new medium in New Zealand, after being recruited by NZBC producer Shirley Maddock.

Later "The Galloping Gourmet," a show named for Kerr's onscreen persona, was taped in Ottawa at CJOH-TV and produced by his wife Treena Kerr. The origin of his "Galloping Gourmet" persona stemmed from a 1967 book he co-authored with wine expert Len Evans, *The Galloping Gourmets.* They got their nickname from a thirty-five-day worldwide trek to the finest restaurants around the globe. The title was echoed in the opening of each episode of his original North American series, filmed in front of a live audience, where Kerr entered the stage area by running in and leaping over a chair in the dining room set.

The series was known for its lighthearted humor, tomfoolery and the copious use of clarified butter, cream and fat. Indeed, Graham's most famous line on the show might have been his response to someone's criticism of his cooking: "Madame, you could go outside and get run over by a bus and just think what you would have missed!" Graham also liberally featured wine, serving it with most meals, drinking it while cooking, using it in his dishes, and waxing poetic about its virtues. In an ongoing feature of the show, Kerr would make his way into the audience as the closing credits began and select an audience member (usually female) whom he would invite onstage with him to enjoy whatever dish he had just prepared. During "The Galloping Gourmet"'s successful run, Graham became a worldwide sensation, wrote an abundance of cookbooks, and earned two Emmy Award nominations. One particularly amusing episode featured Kerr making the British dessert known as "Spotted Dick."[2]

Kerr and Smith, along with Justin Wilson, were the real predecessors of all the numerous cooking shows on TV today, especially on the Cooking Channel. They paved the way for the Iron Chef and many others. Somehow, despite all the clarified butter and wine, Kerr is still alive and active. It is no accident that the rise in popularity of such chefs and shows parallels the rise of obesity in North America particularly. Cooking may be an art and produce some joy, but if one indulges too much in this art, one can quickly become as temporary as last night's meal. Cooking as an art gives the lie to the old Latin proverb "ars longa, vita brevis," for this art does not last very long, and ironically it can shorten your life if you consume too much of it.

Overeating and overdrinking, which is to say gluttony, once described as one of the seven deadly sins, is now seen as the guilty pleasure of choice, even by many Christians. *What is remarkable is that Christians' views on food and drink very seldom have any basis in what the Bible has to say about such subjects.* We have talked about what the Bible says about feasting in general, and we will turn to fasting in a moment. But here would be a good place to talk about what the Bible actually says about drinking alcoholic beverages.

We can gather without too much reflection that the prohibitions on drunkenness are clear enough and don't require debate or discussion. Overindulgence of wine is in fact specifically prohibited for ministers. 1 Timothy 3:3, for example, says that an elder should not be given to drunkenness, or to put it more quaintly, "not given to much wine" (the old term being a "winebibber"). What is not prohibited here or elsewhere in the Bible is the drinking of wine. Indeed, it is endorsed by Paul for medicinal purposes. "Stop drinking water and take a little wine for your stomach," says

2. Accessed June 25, 2011.

1 Timothy 5:23. And yes, there can be little doubt that the wine referred to in the Bible had a certain percentage of alcohol in it; otherwise there would be no warnings about the dangers of becoming a winebibber or a drunk. What should we make of the famous wedding feast at Cana story in John 2?

Despite all sorts of exegetical gymnastics, it is not really possible to avoid the conclusion that Jesus turned water into alcoholic wine at this wedding feast. Early Jews had no moral issues with drinking alcoholic wine, and a Jewish toastmaster at a Jewish wedding would never have said, "Why did you save the best grape juice until last?" The standing joke about Methodists (I'm one myself) is that Jesus turned the water into wine, and ever since Methodists have been trying to turn it back into grape juice. Jesus had no such scruples against wine.

What the toastmaster is in fact talking about is not merely that the most flavorful wine was saved until last, but that the least watered-down wine was served last. The normal ancient practice was to start with the un-watered wine while the palette was still discriminating, and then as the meal went on, the wine served would be more and more watered down. This is the opposite of what happened at the wedding feast of Cana.

It should be added as well that drinking wine in the biblical world was not just because there was little potable water. Making wine was not just a prudential matter, or a matter of necessity so people would have something safe to drink. Cultivating vineyards and making wine was a practice accepted and endorsed by Jews, including various writers of the Old Testament. Psalm 104:14-15, for example, says that the Lord himself "makes grass for cattle, and plants for people to cultivate, bringing forth food from the earth: and wine that gladdens human hearts." The psalmist sees God as the source of food and wine ultimately, and sees it as a good thing. Ecclesiastes 10:19 suggests something similar.

The website www.justforcatholics.org has this to say about the matter under the heading "Wine Is God's Gift":

There are many casual references to wine in the Bible, which suggest that making and drinking wine was a normal aspect of Hebrew culture. For example, Melchizedek brought bread and wine to Abraham and his men — an evidently good deed. Similarly, Jesus spoke of wine, old and new wineskins, vineyards and winepresses in his parables (Matthew 9:17; 21:33). Christ performed his first miracle by changing water into wine (Gk *oinos*) during the wedding feast at Cana (John 2:9).

Some people argue that the Hebrew and Greek words *yayin* and *oinos* (translated "wine") could refer to grape juice as well as fermented wine. However, it is highly unlikely that "wine" is fermented whenever the word is used in a negative context and always unfermented grape juice when used in a positive context! *"Yayin"* and *"oinos"* simply mean wine — containing enough alcohol to cause drunkenness if taken in excess (e.g., "Noah awoke from his wine [*yayin*]" Genesis 9:24; "be not drunk with wine [*oinos*]" Ephesians 5:18).

There are alternative words in Hebrew and Greek meaning "new wine" *(tirosh, gleukos)* — unfermented grape juice or low in alcohol content, or simply wine that is not fully aged. We should keep in mind that once the grapes are crushed, fermentation starts immediately and the juice quickly changes to wine. The alcohol content reaches its near maximum level within a couple of weeks. The Jews did not know of any process (pasteurization was discovered in the nineteenth century) that could prevent grape juice from fermentation.

There is historical evidence that wine was often drunk mixed with water. Some argue that the Jews drank diluted wine because their water supply was polluted (and since clean water is readily available today, they argue, we have no good reason to drink wine). However, that was certainly not the only reason, for the Bible also says that God's people drank wine to make their heart glad and merry. The following scriptures teach that wine is a blessing, a gift of God for our enjoyment.

The website goes on to cite Ecclesiastes 9:7; Psalm 104:14, 15; Deuteronomy 14:26; Amos 9:14; Isaiah 55:1; and Song of Solomon 4:10 before concluding, "Wine is a gift of God. We should not call evil what God, in Scripture, has declared to be good."

This summary is helpful, and basically correct. Drinking wine is condemned in the Bible only when done in excess. It is true that we know today that some people have a natural propensity towards alcoholism. And in a nation full of alcoholics and overindulgers in other sorts of drugs as well, it is understandable that a person committed to biblical holiness would (1) avoid drunkenness altogether; (2) think twice about public drinking, especially in front of people who may have no tolerance for alcohol, especially young people; and (3) may conclude that abstinence is the best policy in general, including for some health reasons. On the other hand, various people with prolapsing mitral valves have been encouraged by doctors to consume red wine with its tannins, as it helps to regulate the heart defect. If you can take a little wine for your stomach, you can take a little for your heart as well. In short, this is one of those *adiaphora* (things indifferent) issues that Paul talks about, and the basic rule of thumb is this: Whatever Christians cannot do in good conscience they should not do. *For them,* it would be a sin to do it, if they cannot do it in good conscience. "Whatever is not of faith, is sin," says St. Paul. He also adds about these sorts of issues on which Christians can agree to disagree, "let each be persuaded in their own minds."

Fasting

It is interesting that the New Testament says very little about the disciples of Jesus fasting. It is certainly not prohibited, but it is also not much endorsed, again except for special reasons and on special occasions. You would never know this from the history of

Christianity, because asceticism seems to have latched on to Christianity already by the second century A.D. and became a mainstay of the monastic movement. Mark Copeland offers an interesting overview on fasting in the New Testament after admitting that *the only fast commanded in the Old Testament is the Day of Atonement fast.*

I. Fasting in the Life of Jesus
   A. Jesus fasted forty days in the wilderness — Matt. 4:1-9; Luke 4:1-2
      1. He was led into the wilderness "to be tempted" (Matt.)
      2. He was "tempted for forty days by the devil" (Luke)
      3. "In those days He ate nothing" (Luke)
         Throughout this forty-day period of temptation, Jesus felt it appropriate to fast
   B. Jesus Taught on Fasting in His "Sermon on the Mount" — Matt. 6:16-18
      1. Jesus said "when," not "if"; assuming his disciples WOULD fast
      2. When done properly a person would be rewarded by the Father . . .
         a. Suggesting that fasting was like prayer and giving alms
         b. I.e., an act of righteousness done to please the Father
            Fasting appears to have a place in the righteousness expected of those who would be citizens of the kingdom of heaven
   C. When Questioned by John's Disciples — Matt. 9:14-17 (Mark 2:18-20; Luke 5:33-39)
      1. Jesus described a time when his disciples would fast
      2. But it is inappropriate to fast when the occasion does not call for it
         Fasting would have a place in the disciples' lives, but

only on appropriate occasions (not as a ceremonial rite)

D. The Combined Power of Prayer and Fasting — Matt. 17:14-21 (Mark 9:14-29)

1. There are times when faith alone is not enough

2. At these times prayer joined with fasting is necessary

Fasting joined with prayer may accomplish things which normal faith may not

II. Fasting in the Lord's Church

A. The Church at Antioch — Acts 13:1-3

1. They were fasting as a group while ministering to the Lord

2. They fasted and prayed in preparation to sending out Barnabas and Saul

Fasting, when accompanied with prayer, can be done as a group when involved in serving the Lord

B. The Churches in Galatia — Acts 14:21-23

1. Again, an example of fasting and prayer as a group; this time, in conjunction with the serious task of appointing elders

2. Notice that this was done *"in every church"*

a. Not just in one or two churches

b. Not just in what might be considered "Jewish" churches where fasting might be considered "just a Jewish custom"

Again, fasting can be a group activity in the work of a local church

III. Fasting in the Ministry of the Apostle Paul

A. Fasting Was a Mark of His Ministry . . .

1. We have already noticed where he fasted with several churches

2. But notice also:

a. 2 Cor. 6:4-10 (cf. v. 5)

b. 2 Cor. 11:23-28 (cf. v. 27 where fasting is mentioned separately from normal hunger and thirst)
In both of these passages, Paul mentioned fasting as a mark of his ministry and of his good standing as a minister of Christ!

B. He Also Taught That Fasting Might Have a Place in the Lives of Others . . .

1. Cf. 1 Cor. 7:5

2. The only time husbands and wives may deprive one another is when by consent they devote themselves to fasting and prayer for a specific period of time

Conclusion

1. Though not actually Christians at the time, we also have other examples of those who fasted and were blessed by God . . .

   a. Anna — Luke 2:36-38

   b. Saul — Acts 9:9

   c. Cornelius — Acts 10:30-31

2. As a summary, then, here is what we have seen in this study:

   a. That our Lord fasted in time of temptation

   b. That He taught His disciples about fasting on several occasions

   c. That He foretold of a time in which His disciples would fast

   d. That there are times when the combination of fasting and prayer might be more efficacious than prayer alone

   e. That the early church fasted in their service to the Lord

   f. That Paul regarded fasting as a mark of his ministry

   g. That prayer and fasting often go hand in hand, utilized whenever there was a strong desire for God's blessing and guidance

In view of such things, I can only conclude that fasting does indeed have a place in the lives of Christians today.[3]

I think this summary is basically correct. What it shows, however, is that *fasting is not the same thing as dieting*. In each of the cases cited by Copeland we are talking about fasting for religious purposes, but as he says, *not* for purely ceremonial purposes, and certainly not as a way to display one's piety to others. Fasting is undertaken often in tandem with prayer when (1) there is a crisis, or (2) a major decision must be made, or (3) one is attempting to heal someone, or (4) one needs to draw especially close to God at some point and listen to God. One of the most interesting references to fasting is the connection between fasting and exorcism in one of the sayings of Jesus. Fasting shows one's seriousness and commitment to getting something accomplished; in particular it is done to demonstrate to God one's earnestness about something.

One fast that I have found spiritually nourishing during Holy Week is fasting from Maundy Thursday night until Easter Sunday morning. The basis for this is not only to honor and focus on what Christ did for us on the cross, but also to honor what Jesus said at the Last Supper — that he had longed to take the meal with his disciples, but in regard to the cup of wine — "I will not drink it again, until I drink anew in the Kingdom." As Jesus had said earlier, there was a time for mourning and fasting, when the Bridegroom was no longer with them, and so a fast is appropriate both in this way during Holy Week, but also during Lent in general when we focus on Christ's journey to Golgotha and the things he sacrificed on our behalf. I would stress again that fasting for religious purposes is not the same as simply dieting, though there are plenty of good reasons to do the latter if one is overweight. Obe-

3. This comes from his Executable Outlines on his website http://www .executableoutlines.com, accessed June 25, 2011.

sity is simply a terrible witness to the world. If we do not take care of our bodies as a sign that we know they are a gift from God, why should anyone listen to us when we talk about the body being God's temple?

The Normal Christian Life of Someone Who Is a Light to the World

One of the books that most impacted me during seminary was Ron Sider's classic, *Rich Christians in an Age of Hunger*.[4] This book served as a wakeup call to me personally that I needed to be concerned about the 1.2 billion persons who live in poverty. And one of the things I needed to be most concerned with was my own wasting of food, as well as indulging in various sorts of foods that were not good for me. Sider raised the consciousness of all of us when it came to caring about the poor, and how our own conduct in regard to food and drink can either be a good witness or a bad one, either a witness that shows we care about the poor, or that we really don't much care about them. I began to realize that even our decisions about basic things in life such as eating and drinking needed to come under the searchlight of Christ.

Eating and drinking are not condemned in the Bible per se, but in fact it is not just overindulgence that is critiqued. A thoughtless, self-centered, self-indulgent attitude about life in general is critiqued, and this affects the way we should view our eating and drinking. While Christians are not called to be buzz-kills or killjoys, and there are special occasions to enjoy feasting with friends and/or family and/or brothers and sisters in Christ, we must bear in mind that God calls us to (1) take care of ourselves, which includes proper diet and exercise; (2) care about the

4. InterVarsity, 1977. As of 2005, there is a revised and updated version published by Thomas Nelson.

poor, and do something practical about that sense of compassion; (3) be a good witness to others that the body is a gift from God and indeed the dwelling place of God's spirit. There is something inherently sacred or sacrilegious about what we do with the body, and without question gluttony is a sin condemned in the Bible.

What I am really talking about here is being a global and mission-minded Christian. If you have worked in poor countries in the world, as I have from time to time, you see how the other half lives. Indeed, you can see this in towns all over America if you just look. It's not just, as John Donne put it, that "every man's death diminishes me, for I am a part of mankind"; it's that Jesus loves and died for all the peoples of the world. We, therefore, have an obligation to care about their plight, to show compassion, and to live in a way that frees up resources so we can help the poor. One way to do that is to stop spending so much on ourselves, including on food and drink for ourselves. What we do with our so-called discretionary income speaks volumes about our priorities in life. "To whom more is given, more is required," says the Bible, and this includes those of us who are not wealthy by American standards, but by world standards are actually rich and spoiled and pampered.[5]

What is needed in the twenty-first century is Christians who realize, as Wesley once said, that there is no spiritual holiness without social holiness, and vice versa. We need more Christians who are both spiritually formed and socially motivated. We need Christians who consciously think through their lives and de-enculturate themselves from many of the values of the dominant Western culture, including consumerism and conspicuous consumption, not to mention the disease of the health and wealth gospel. The only health gospel a Christian should be preaching is healthy eating and healthy living, including a commitment to a

---

5. See Witherington, *Jesus and Money: A Guide for Times of Financial Crisis* (Grand Rapids: Brazos, 2010).

nutritious diet and regular exercise. This should be the norm for Christians everywhere.

One of the things that perhaps most needs to be discarded is the *aesthetic* approach to food. By this I mean that you decide what you eat on the basis of "what tastes good to me." I am not opposed to eating tasty food. It's preferable to food that tastes like cardboard. But the decision about what you eat should not mainly be based on mere preference or "how it tastes to me." The first criteria should be — "Is it good for me, and if so, in what quantities?" Even worse is the see food diet — if people see food, they eat it. They are ruled by their appetites, and it doesn't much matter what sort of food is set in front of them.

A self-conscious Christian seeking to make ethical decisions about food will need (1) to be aware of what one's own metabolic rate is; (2) to know what foods one may be allergic to; (3) to understand what a proper food pyramid looks like for one in terms of portions of fruit, vegetables, fish, meat, bread, juices, etc.; (4) to know how many calories one burns by work and normal exercise in a given day (the intake should not regularly exceed what is being burned up); and (5) as one's body changes with age, to consult a nutritionist about decreasing intake of certain things, and increasing other things, and whether one needs to take vitamin supplements. It is precisely this sort of "take control of your diet and exercise" approach that is needed, perhaps especially with ministers, who have so many external stressors in their lives. One's effectiveness and longevity in ministry will in part be decided on the basis of whether one deals with these sorts of basic health issues.

There are simple steps one can take to have a more appropriate approach to eating. Nutritionist Steve Elbert says, "We think fast food is equivalent to pornography, nutritionally speaking." If you haven't seen the documentary "Super-Size Me," about a healthy young man who ate nothing but fast food for a month or so (and gained almost a pound a day, with his cholesterol and triglycerides going out of sight), you should watch it online. It reminds us that some things should be eaten rarely, if at all. And most fast food falls into this category. Once you've gotten past those sorts of regular temptations, then it is time to also bear in mind that when you are eating out, you should avoid taking more than you can normally eat. Avoid buffet-line restaurants altogether if possible, especially if your eyes are bigger than your stomach (though your stomach keeps growing).

Eating these days needs to be done in consultation with one's doctor, to determine whether one is fighting a lot of heredity. Many of us are, and knowing this can help us outline the sorts of foods and snacks and the like that we should regularly avoid. The problem is the psychological side of eating, which Christians too seldom take into account. We readily talk about *comfort* food, but if comfort food as compensation for something else means something like a Twinkie, we need to find another source of comfort. I have yet to meet a person who ate carrots as comfort food. It is true that our moods and psychological state affect our eating patterns. Some people eat much more when they are depressed; some do just the opposite. You need to know and monitor your own tendencies as well as your own temptations. There is a famous story told about Oscar Wilde at a London party. A servant came by with a plate of bonbons. "Mr. Wilde," she said, "can I tempt you with a bonbon?" His reply was, "Madam, I can resist anything but temptation." Unfortunately it is the story of too many Christians.

It is sad but true that people eat because of disappointments, they eat because they think no one loves them, they eat because they have ceased caring about what they look like, they eat because they don't get any sex. *But eating was not intended to serve the purpose of a therapist or a mate or a doctor.* It was intended to take care of a basic need we have to go on living. It is not wrong to enjoy eating, and feast once in a while, and occasionally eat things that on a regular basis would not be good for you. The issue here is what one's regular or normal pattern of life is. Are you glorifying God, edifying yourself, and bearing good witness to others by how and what and when and how much you eat? If not, you need to begin to think about it. You may even need to study yourself and your habits and patterns and lifestyle and the whole eating and drinking matter more closely. And as we have seen in this chapter, the Bible has a good deal to say to help us with these matters. But we need to end this discussion by talking about the Kingdom perspective.

Jesus tells us that we had best practice hospitality now, as the day is coming when the messianic banquet is going to involve our sitting down with a whole bunch of unfamiliar dinner guests. There are several texts that talk about the coming Kingdom as involving eating and drinking and a celebratory feast. We may think of the parable of the wedding banquet in Matthew 22:1-14, or we could examine the parable of the wise and foolish virgins in Matthew 25:1-14, but instead I want to focus on Jesus' actual description, outside of a parable, of the coming Kingdom. The context of Matthew 8:11-12 is that Jesus has done a good deed for a centurion, a pagan, and his Jewish followers are amazed. In this context Jesus adds, "I say to you that many will come from the east and the west, and will take their places at the feast with Abraham, Isaac, and Jacob in the kingdom of heaven. But the subjects of the kingdom will be thrown outside, into the darkness, where there will be weeping and gnashing of teeth." Some who we would expect to be in, from an early Jewish point of view, will be out, and vice versa. This saying reminds us not merely that there will be unexpected Gentiles coming to dinner, but also there will be patriarchs who at least in their former lives were not card-carrying followers of Jesus.

In order to fully understand the import of this saying we must remember the very high value placed on hospitality even to strangers, even to enemies in the ancient Near East, including Jewish culture. Psalm 23 itself warned that God might arrange a strange dinner guest for the psalmist himself — "You prepare a table for me in the presence of my enemies." God's version of "Guess Who's Coming to Dinner?" proves to be as surprising as the 1960s movie of the same name. For our purposes what is important is not merely the surprising guest list, but the fact that Jesus expects eating and drinking to be one of the things that will characterize life in the future Kingdom on earth when he returns. There may be no more marrying and giving in marriage in the Kingdom, but there will be eating and drinking. Why?

Because meals are one of the main ways communion and koinonia happen and intimate relationships are built. *Eating was meant to be a social activity,* not merely a private indulgence. It was meant to build community, not just meet our individual needs. Eugene Peterson in his wonderful book *Reversed Thunder* stresses that when the Kingdom comes we will not only have all we need, but we will only want exactly what we have. In the meantime we need to cultivate a theology of enough, of what is sufficient, and do the hard work of distinguishing between our appetites and wants on the one hand, and what we actually need on the other.

The industrial revolution and indeed the technology revolution have not been kind to us in various ways when it comes to being fit and healthy Christians. Many of us, both in our work and in our leisure, have become couch potatoes for Jesus. The industrial revolution changed America from a country in which 66 percent of people lived on farms in 1900 to a country in which only about 6 percent lived on farms in 2000. No wonder when children are asked at school where food comes from they say, "from the grocery store," not "from the farm." We have bought the myth that we have infinite resources ("eat all you want; we'll make more") and then get frustrated when we run out of things. But eating and drinking should constantly remind us that we are mortal and need fuel regularly, and that we are going to constantly run out of contingent resources like food and drink. Jesus alone gives a drink that doesn't leave us thirsty and bread that feeds forever.

In Sum

At the end of the day, eating is a sign that we want to go on living. Notice what happens to a person when they lose "the will to go on living." They stop eating. Most of the time, most of us want life, and we want it abundantly. But the life we most need, food and drink can't provide. The God-shaped vacuum in the human heart cannot be filled with physical food. "Taste and see that the Lord is good," say the Scriptures. In the next chapter we must talk about a very different sort and source of nourishment — studying the Scriptures. As we shall see, eating a book is a different sort of task than eating a burger, and it provides a different sort of sustenance. It is, however, just as necessary or even more necessary for the normal Christian life. For now I leave you with this thought courtesy of Jesus: "Eat, drink, and be merry while the Bridegroom is with you, for tomorrow you may live forever."

CHAPTER FOUR

Eat This Book — Studying the Scriptures

I am a spirit come from God and returning to God. . . . I want to know one thing, the way to heaven. . . . God Himself has condescended to teach me the way. . . . He has written it down in a book. O give me that book! At any price, give me the book of God! I have it: here is knowledge enough for me. Let me be homo unius libri [a man of one book]. Here then I am, far from the busy ways of men. I sit down alone. Only God is here. In His presence I open, I read His book; for this end, to find the way to Heaven.

John Wesley

Study — The Problem

I have, in the last decade or so, spent a lot of time exhorting my seminary students to please commit themselves to lifelong learning. I've used all the best rhetoric to hand, stressed the importance of this, made required reading in my courses a minimum for passing the course to get them jump-started, and still many of them will not do much reading. As it turns out, much too much of the computer generation doesn't want to read, unless it's soundbites and McNuggets in the form of Facebook posts, tweets, and the occasional article online. Sadly, many of them don't trust information they can't find online, when it ought to be the other way around. There is a reason much of the free stuff online is free.

Many of my students don't even want Kindles. So what can I do to kindle their interest in study? I've resorted to using film clips and the like. I realize most of them are basically visual learners, so I understand the need for visual stimuli. But at some point, they have to bite the bullet and actually read a book. And from my point of view they need to start with the Bible itself. It is shocking to see how many seminary students are biblically illiterate and blithely unaware of the significance of this deficiency. I usually try a little experiment in the first class of the basic New Testament Intro. I ask them all to turn to the book of Hezekiah, and then I watch to see how many are frantically paging through the Old Testament. Alas, far too many of them. I suspect that when I hear them muttering about all the reading I assign, they are saying "of the making of books there is no end, and much reading is a weariness of the flesh." But some books are more important than others, the Bible being the chief of these.

Why is lifelong learning and the study of God's Word in particular so important? Suppose I were to ask the question: Why is it important to know God and his Son and the Spirit? Might that stir a bit more urgency in the heart? The truth is, you cannot know God in any adequate way without studying God's love letter to us — the Bible. Unlike our own personal spiritual experiences, which are often difficult to interpret or make sense of because of their profound subjectivity, the Bible, like God's creation, is an *objective* source through which we can know God, and not merely know *about* God. And the reason for this is simple. The Bible is not just another book; it is the living Word of God. If you want to know the living God, you need to know the living Word of God; and like God, on a smaller scale, it takes a lifetime to understand the complexities of the Bible. Trust me, I know. I'm still working on it, and since I'd like to have Jesus find my name in the Lamb's book of everlasting life when the Kingdom comes, I am studying away on this earthly book that God left us.

"Study to Show Yourself Approved"

It's the advice of an aging Christian to one of his understudies. He's far away from his young friend and fellow Christian minister, and frankly he's worried about him. He gives him lots of good advice, and one of the more salient points he makes is this: "Do your best to present yourself to God as one approved, a worker who does not need to be ashamed and who correctly handles the word of truth" (2 Tim. 2:15). This verse is often used to encourage people to engage in Bible study (even though if Paul were talking about a Bible here, it would have been just the Old Testament). But Bible study is one thing; reading the Bible with the same openness to it as a living Word, as one is open to the living God, is another.

Here is a fuller and more literal citation of the whole context of 2 Timothy 2:15:

> Call this to mind, adjuring [people] before God not to engage in word battles about nothing useful unto the ruin of the hearers. Be eager to present yourself approved to God, a workman with nothing to be ashamed of, cutting straight the word of truth, but avoiding godless chatter, for they make even more progress in godlessness, and their word like gangrene will eat its way. Hymenaeus and Philetus are among them. These sorts of folk are wide of the mark concerning the truth, saying the resurrection has already happened and unsettling the faith of some. The firm foundation of God, however, stands.

Let us consider these verses in more detail. At verse 14 Paul turns to the issue of the false teachers. Notice how there is the call for Timothy to remember these things. He is urged not to get sucked into the war of words (word battles; see 1 Tim. 6:4) and disputes, which accomplish nothing useful and in fact may lead to the ruination of the listeners. In other words, Timothy is not to stoop to the tactics and mode of rhetorical discourse of the opponents, who earlier in 1 Timothy are said to engage in such fruitless word battles. Our author is arguing in a deliberative fashion, showing that verbal battles result in no advantage or nothing useful or beneficial.

Instead, verse 15 urges that Timothy present himself to God as an approved workman of God with nothing to be ashamed of. Ancient moralists believed that unless character is tested and proved, it cannot be assumed to be mature or reliable (cf. Epictetus, *Fragments* 28b, 112; Prov. 27:21; Sir. 2:1). This may mean a person not ashamed of the job he has to do. The last phrase in verse 15 is highly debated: "he is to cut straight the word of God." The verb *orthotomounta* is an interesting one, found only here in the New Testament. It refers to the cutting of a path or road (see Prov. 3:6; 11:5 LXX; Plato, *Laws* 810E), or the cutting of a stone. Probably what is meant here is not "rightly dividing the Scriptures," but rather cutting straight to the point in one's preaching, proclaiming the straight stuff, not beating around the bush with esoterica, unlike the false teachers (cf. Gal. 2:14). This view is supported by what follows in verse 16 with the comments about avoiding godless talk or specious reasoning (see 1 Tim. 6:20). It is also supported by recognizing that *orthopoeia* is a rhetorical term referring to the quality of exactness or precision, without flaw or error. Timothy is to speak directly and clearly about the words of truth, or — as we might say — "cut to the chase" or get to the point.

Those who are doing some of these ill-advised things are advancing (*prokoptein* — to advance in the sense of make progress; see Rom. 13:12; Gal. 1:14; 1 Tim. 4:15; 2 Tim. 3:9, 13) in godlessness, not godliness. This is probably intended as irony, since the opponents seem to have thought they were offering the advanced teaching. Paul's response is, "They are progressing all right, but in the wrong direction." Their words are like gangrene finding some tender flesh to feast on and eating away at the fiber of someone's faith (cf. Hippocrates, *On Joints* 63). Paul names names here — Hymenaeus and Philetus are among the false teachers who deny the resurrection.

What we learn from these verses is something of the reason why study is important — namely, what we believe about God, and salvation, and resurrection *matters*. If in the last chapter we learned that to some extent "you are what you eat," here we learn that "you are what you study and learn." While this passage is not actually about rightly studying the Bible, but rather about rightly presenting its truth, cutting to the chase and being clear, nevertheless it presupposes such study. You can't teach what you don't know, and you can't teach clearly what you don't clearly understand yourself. And in some ways, the Bible is the deepest and most complex book there is. I am not saying it is not perspicuous; I am saying that all too often our own understanding of it is quite cloudy. We haven't the foggiest notion of what some of it really means.

Devouring the Word

Psalm 119 is a truly remarkable acrostic poem, ringing the changes on the letters of the Hebrew alphabet in alphabetical order. One could call this little song "How to Learn the Word from A to Z." A few words of background are necessary to understand this psalm. The author is basically talking about Torah proper — by which I mean the Mosaic Laws. He rings the changes on the words "law," "precepts," "statutes," "commandments," "ordinances" throughout this song. Some Christians may find it puzzling that someone would wax eloquent about the Law, but this is precisely what is going on in the psalm. This man is in love with God's Law, has fully embraced it, and is doing all he can to obey it. The psalm does not depict a person who finds the Law a huge burden, nor a person who should be called a "legalist" or a legalistic nitpicker. On the contrary, he sees these laws as the living Word of God and embraces them in the same way he embraces his God, and, as he says, they are the joy of his heart. Seeking God has to do with keeping commandments.

Our interest in the psalm has to do with how the author approaches Torah, how he studies it. Let us start with verse 11: "I have hidden your word in my heart." The author is talking about internalizing God's Word, and the basic form of ancient education involved memorization and oral recitation. You can still see this today at the Wailing Wall in Jerusalem. Torah students have memorized various passages, and they recite these passages out loud over and over again as a way of praying to God and relating to God. Though modern education has gotten away from memorization of things, this is not necessarily a good thing. Let me tell you one of my favorite Fred Craddock stories.

Fred was professor of New Testament and Preaching at Emory for many years. One morning a disheveled-looking young student stumbled into his office looking for help. He asked her to sit down and to tell her story. She began to relate how the previous night she had resolved to end her life, by jumping off a train trestle into a nearby shallow river. She then said that when she got up on the abutment to jump she heard a voice inside her say, "Be still, and know that I am God." This frightened her, and she backed away from the precipice and came back to her dorm a mess. After a sleepless night, she came to see Dr. Craddock. After she told her story, he asked her a series of questions: "Are you a Christian?" "No," came the reply. "Have you read the Bible?" "No," came the reply. "Do you ever go to church?" "No," came the reply. But then she stopped and said, "Well, when I was a little girl my grandmother took me to some special summer church thing — vacation something school." Dr. Craddock asked her what she remembered about it. "Well, I remember cutting out little strips of paper with my silver scissors, and writing words on them, and then getting up in front of the group and reciting the words." "Aha," said Dr. Craddock. "Those words were surely Bible verses, and one of them lodged in your heart and just saved your life!"

The psalmist says he has hidden God's Word in his heart, a place where no one can take it away from him. But notice he says why he has done so — "so that I might not sin against you." This is not Scripture memorization for its own sake. This is Scripture memorization for salvation's sake, for a practical and ethical end. Notice in verse 13 the reference to reciting God's Word out loud ("with my lips . . ."). Then in verse 15 we have the word "meditate," which is a different Hebrew word here than the one sometimes translated "ruminate" in Psalm 1. The verb in verse 15 refers to pondering or reflecting on something at length. It is not talking about any sort of medieval or modern meditation practices, such as *lectio divina,* though this psalm could be used that way. The author is saying that the diligent believer should (1) memorize and recite God's commands, and (2) reflect deeply on their meaning; but that is by no means all. The function of studying God's Word is not merely to understand it but, as the psalmist says, to delight in it, to rejoice in it, and finally to walk in it. Study is not an end in itself; it is a means to an end, the end being both obedience to God's Word and drawing closer to God himself.

Despite the intense effort at learning God's Word, the psalmist in verses 33-34 still beseeches God to teach him and give him understanding, whoever his human teachers may have been. There are issues of the heart that only God can deal with. Not only does God give true understanding; verses 36-37 petition God to turn the psalmist's heart towards the commandments and turn his eyes away from worthless things. In verse 41 he also prays that God's love will come his way, and he asks in verse 43 that God not take his word of truth out of the psalmist's mouth. According to verse 66, what comes with knowledge is also good judgment about life's issues. The Word of God is also studied in order to make practical decisions about life. This is why in the famous verse 105 the psalmist says that God's Word is a lamp unto his feet, which is to say, it sheds light on the path he should take in life. It is never a case of relevance when it comes to God's Word. The psalmist believes God's Word is not merely eternal, but eternally relevant as well. He also believes that God's Word is holy and righteous and good (vv. 160, 164).

If one reads carefully the whole psalm, especially the last six or so stanzas, one of the things that becomes evident is that the psalmist has great reverence for God's Word (notice the verb "tremble" in v. 161), but he is claiming and standing on the promises in God's Word, hence he calls God to rescue him and fulfill the previous promises he made about salvation of his people. The encounter with God in God's Word leads ultimately to doxology — to the praise of God for teaching the psalmist his word (v. 171).

The companion wisdom psalm is Psalm 19, and it deserves our attention at this point. Our concern is with verses 7-14. The first half of the song is about the book of nature as God's word-less Word, as his general revelation, making known who he is. The second half, however, is on God's written or special revelation, and again the specific focus is on his Law, which may have been the first portion of God's Word ever written down. Certainly the ten commandments are said to have been personally inscribed on stone by God himself. This gives new meaning to an inspired word from God — God's handwritten commands to his people.

Psalm 19 tells us a good deal of the effects of God's Word once it is studied, learned, imbibed, chewed on, meditated on, and sung. The author says that God's living word revives or refreshes the soul (v. 7). Far from being death-dealing, the commandments are life-giving. Verse 7b says that even the simple become wise when they learn the Word. They also give joy to the heart and light to the eyes. In the famous verse 10 we are told that tasting or taking in God's Word is like eating honey; indeed it is sweeter than honey.

Taken together, Palms 119 and 19 make evident that deep meditation on and learning of God's Word are a key to (1) gaining wisdom, (2) figuring out what direction your life should go in, (3) spiritual renewal, and (4) having joy in your life. But implicit in all of this is that one's relationship with God and the health of one's relationship with God is closely linked to the studying and learning of God's Word. The psalmist also suggests that there are rewards for keeping God's Word. He doesn't assume that virtue is its own reward.

One might get the impression from a close examination of Psalms 19 and 119 that studying God's Word is a private matter — just you and your Bible. This would be a mistake, because these very psalms are not private reflections but part of the sung liturgy of Israel, shared by all worshipers. The author assumes that all the audience needs to do such study; it's not just for the learned in their midst. Indeed, the author assumes that this activity is fundamental to being a believer at all, of any kind. And he nowhere suggests that such study is just for beginners, though clearly there are levels of instruction. The goal is not just lifelong learning but becoming mature in the faith and more perfect in one's obedience to God.

It is important to bear in mind that the word we translate as "disciple" in the Gospels, *mathetes,* means literally a learner. When you commit yourself to being a disciple of Jesus, you set yourself on a course of learning God's Word, learning from the words, deeds, and life of Jesus, learning from imitating Christ, and in due course growing up, becoming a person of seasoned understanding and maturity in the faith. Clement of Alexandria reminds us: "Just as we say that it is possible to have faith without being literate, so we assert that it is *not* possible to understand the statements contained in the faith without study. To assimilate the right affirmations and reject the rest is not the product of simple faith but of faith engaged in learning" (*Stromateis* 1.6.35) — or, as Anselm was later to put it, "faith seeking understanding" *(fides quaerens intellectum)*.

On the subject of learning and maturation, the author of Hebrews has much to say. Our focus must be on Hebrews 5:11–6:3 in some real detail, but it is well to remember that the author characterizes all of Hebrews as a "brief" and elementary instruction. Here is what the text says:

> Concerning which the word has much for us, and it is difficult to explain, since your ears have become sluggish. And though you ought to be teachers by this time again you have need of being taught some of the elementary principles of the beginning of the word of God, and you have become [persons] having need of milk, not solid food. For all the partakers of milk without experience of the word of righteousness, are infants. But for the mature there is solid food, and through the training by practice of their faculties, they have ability to distinguish good and evil. So then, leaving behind the word about the beginning/origin of Christ let us move along to completion/maturity/perfection, not laying again the foundation of repentance from dead works and faith in God, teaching about baptisms, the imposition of hands, resurrection of the dead, and eternal judgment.[1]

At 5:11, the outset of the exhortation, our author accuses the audience of being sluggish or dull in their hearing, or as we might put it, being hard of hearing. Notice the oral and aural character of the teaching in this setting. It is much the same as when Jesus repeatedly exhorted his audience, "Let those with two good ears,

1. The discussion that follows here can be found in more detail and in a fuller form in my *Letters and Homilies for Jewish Christians: A Socio-Rhetorical Commentary on Hebrews, James and Jude* (Downers Grove, IL: InterVarsity, 2008).

hear." Our author nevertheless is going to plow ahead and give them more advanced teaching about Christ the heavenly high priest, beginning in the latter part of Hebrews 6. But here he starts with a reminder that the "word" has much to say to his audience, but that doesn't mean it is either easy to explain or easy to understand, especially if one is spiritually deaf, or there are obstacles to one hearing clearly and grasping the implications of what has been heard. We have heard all along that our audience had such hearing deficiencies (see 2:1; 3:7-8, 15; 4:2, 7).

The clarity of the Word is one thing, the acuteness of the hearer quite another. The word *nothros* is found only here and at Hebrews 6:12 in the whole New Testament, and it is the notion that sets off this unit from what follows. Our author in fact may be thinking of the striking passage in Isaiah 50:4-5, which says literally "the Lord God dug out my ear" or as we might say, cleaned the wax out of my ear. When this term is not used of a physical attribute it refers to being dull-witted, timid, negligent (see Polybius, *Histories* 3.63.7; 4.8.5; 4.60.2). Epictetus, for example, rebukes the sluggish who refuse to discipline themselves by using their reason (*Discourses* 1.7.30). To be sluggish in this case is to be slow to hear; it does not quite connote the idea of hardness of heart, though the author fears they may be headed in that direction, perhaps due to outside pressure.

Verse 12 makes the interesting remark that by now the audience ought themselves to be teachers rather than needing to be taught. Seneca complains in a similar way: "How long will you be a learner? From now on, be a teacher as well" (*Moral Letters* 33.8-9). This suggests a situation where we are dealing with a congregation of persons who have been Christians for a considerable period of time, hence the exasperation of the author with the audience. It's time for them to grow up and get on with it. In this verse we see the use of the term *stoicheia*; in fact we have the phrase *"stoicheia tes arches,"* which has caused a good deal of debate. The word *stoicheia* by itself means rudiments, or parts, and can refer to a part of a word (a letter, a syllable — hence the alphabet) or a part of the universe (i.e., an element, an original component). This second possibility is its meaning in Wisdom 7:17; 19:18. There is much debate as to what the *stoicheia tou kosmou* means in Galatians 4:3, 9 and Colossians 2:8, 20, but probably it means elementary teaching. This last meaning especially seems to suit Colossians 2:8. In any case *stoicheia* linked with *arches* surely means first principles, or elementary rudiments of teaching that they had already heard from the beginning of their Christian pilgrimage.

There are parallels where clearly enough it refers to the elementary teaching or principles, not to some elemental spirits or beings (cf. Xenophon, *Memorabilia* 2.1.1). Of even more relevance is the very beginning of Quintilian's famous study on rhetoric where he says, "I would therefore have a father conceive the highest hopes of his son from the moment of his birth. If he does so he will be more careful about the foundation/groundwork of his education. For there is absolutely no foundation for the complaint that but few men have the power to take in the knowledge that is imparted to them, and that the majority are so slow of understanding, that education is a waste of time and labor. On the contrary you will find that most are quick to reason and ready to learn" (*Orator's Education* 1.1.1). In this context the "elementary principles" are the beginnings of instruction in the art of persuasion, presumably some of the elements of the "progymnasmata" program. That our author is trying to shame his audience into learning more is clear enough from the fact that "milk" is for infants, and his audience are adults; or put another way, elementary education was for those between seven and fourteen. It was never flattering to suggest adults were acting like children of that age.

One may wish to ask about verse 13, what is the "word of righteousness," or the teaching about righteousness? One may presume that it has to do with the subject of apostasy, which the writer will dole out a significant dose of in a moment. However, in Greco-

Roman settings instruction in righteousness meant being trained in discerning the difference between good and evil (Xenophon, *Cyropaedia* 1.630-31). In rhetorical contexts, this sort of language referred to reaching a "state" in which they could be rhetors (Quintilian, *Orator's Education* 10.1.1; 10.5.1). Verse 14 identifies Christian maturity with the capacity to distinguish moral good from moral evil, which in turn means being able to continue to pursue the course of righteous action and avoid apostasy.

At 6:1 we have the interesting verb *pherometha,* which can be translated "move along," but it can also mean "be carried along." Both things are actually part of the process of maturing in Christ, and moving toward the goal of moral and intellectual excellence. Our author does not want his audience to forget what they learned at the earlier stages, for example, forgetting to repent when necessary. These things are foundational. Rather, he wants them to move along to more advanced subjects, building on top of the original elementary learning. We have here the term *teleiotes,* which can be translated "maturity," but unlike that English word, the Greek word has the connotation of arriving at a goal or the completion of something one was striving towards, which is why it is sometimes translated "perfection/completion." In this case, the author has in mind an intended eschatological goal and state. The "mature Christian is expected not only to 'ingest' the solid food but also to follow Christ on the path to final perfection, whatever the cost."[2] We should compare Hebrews 3:14 and 6:11.

There is debate as to what we should make of the phrase "the word about the beginning of Christ." This could refer to what our author was talking about in Hebrews 1:1-4, but that does not seem to suit this context. It could also refer to the basic moral teaching of Christ, which according to the summary in Mark 1:15 was "repent and believe the good news." That comports rather nicely

2. H. Attridge, *Hebrews* (Philadelphia: Fortress Press, 1989), p. 215.

with the content of the rest of verse 1. Our author has assumed before now in the discourse a knowledge of the historical Jesus' life on the part of the audience (5:7-8), and presumably this would include some knowledge about his teachings. But is this "beginning" material to be seen as synonymous with "the elementary principles/teachings of the oracles of God" referred to in 5:12?

All the terms that follow *didaches* are likely seen as the content of this teaching. Once again our author must stress that becoming a Christian back then involved not only activities but also believing certain things. There were early catechisms that talked about such matters, and we know that early on there was a sort of probationary period for the catechists. As has been pointed out, there appears to be nothing particularly Christian about these matters. Any good Pharisee could have made up this list, but it is worth noting that Christianity, though it taught about many of the same subjects as the Pharisees, did not take the same view about them. Faith in God, for instance, meant faith in God through Christ, for the Christian. Resurrection meant not just at the end of history, but already in Christ. Imposition of hands in early Judaism, which usually would have been for blessing, or later for ordination of rabbis, in Christianity was connected with receiving the Spirit and/or taking on a work of ministry.

Most commentators have assumed that the list in 6:1-2 refers to the subject matter of elementary Christian teaching, and there can be little doubt that this is correct since our author is stressing that his audience has heard such teaching before and needs to move on to the more advanced teaching. However, something should be said for the generic character of this list of paired opposites here, which could well have been said to be the substance of Jesus' own teaching:

> Repentance from past dead works — faith towards God
> Instructions about baptisms — laying on of hands
> Resurrection of the dead — eternal judgment

There is nothing here that Jesus could not have commented on, especially if we take the reference to baptisms plural to refer either to ritual ablutions or more likely to John's baptism as opposed to that practiced by Jesus' own disciples (see John 3:22; 4:2). The observation that all these topics could have arisen in synagogue teaching is accurate, and some of the audience may have heard of these things in that context first, and even have been tending in a retrograde motion to focus on such things as they sought to move back under the umbrella of early Judaism. There is a certain progression in this list from repentance at the beginning of the Christian life to final judgment at the end, after the resurrection of the dead.

But this is all the more reason to suggest that Jesus commented on and taught about these topics as well. Jesus of course engaged in laying on of hands as well, a practice that could have to do with blessing, healing, or even setting apart for some service or task, and he certainly spoke about coming judgment as well as the coming resurrection of the dead. What we could then have here is a shorthand of the elementary teaching of Jesus that was taken over into the elementary teaching of the church and called "the beginning of the word/teaching of Jesus." We may wish to contrast what we find in 10:22, where clearly enough it is not the water ritual that cleanses the conscience, but rather the internal application of grace by the Spirit resulting from the shed blood of Christ. Whether we see this elementary teaching as essentially Jewish or essentially Christian or both, it is something our author wants the audience to move beyond as they grow towards maturity.

Now anyone who has read the sermon called Hebrews straight through even once knows that in fact our author expects quite a lot out of his audience when it comes to study and learning, listening and learning, and he is in no way satisfied with, or allowing his audience to be satisfied with, just believing and knowing the things that can turn them into a Christian in the first place. To the contrary, he is arguing that they must commit themselves to ongoing learning, to going higher up and deeper into Christian teaching and God's Word, and his fear is that instead of moving towards Christian maturity by further learning, they are in danger of going in a retrograde direction.

It is sadly the case today that there are many Christians in an arrested state of spiritual and intellectual and emotional infancy when it comes to the Christian faith and knowing God's Word. Our author is arguing vigorously that it is not enough to simply gain right standing with God; one's spiritual growth and health after one's conversion are crucial and necessary if one is to not only go on to maturity, but avoid apostasy, and one day follow Christ into the Kingdom (see Heb. 12:1-4).

Study affects one's spiritual health, and indeed it also has something to do with one's final salvation, according to the author of Hebrews, or at least it helps one avoid apostasy. More study, more learning is not an optional added extra for the more zealous Christians alone. If there is one lesson a pastor today should learn from Hebrews it is this — that it is not his job to boil down the gospel to pablum or infant's formula. It is his job to boil up the people and fire them up to growth in Christ, through learning more about God's Word and about their faith. Furthermore, it is his responsibility to set a good example in regard to lifelong learning, and indeed to share what he is learning in mature Christian teaching and preaching. If sermons today were actually more like Hebrews, which is a single sermon, there would probably be a whole lot fewer immature and biblically illiterate Christians in our churches.

Study in an Oral Culture

One of the things we are often guilty of when it comes to reading the Bible is assuming that those cultures were like our cultures when it came to texts. In fact this is not true. The biblical cultures seem to have had a literacy rate of about 15 percent at most, if by literacy we mean those who could write. If we include those who could read to some degree, but depended on scribes to write, we might get up to a quarter of the population at most. The proper question that we should ask about texts like Psalm 119 or 19 or Hebrews 5–6 is: How do sacred texts function in a largely oral culture, and how did people learn if they couldn't both read and write?

In an ancient oral culture, learning and studying did not amount to burying oneself in papyri and reading away. Most people couldn't do that. It was not just that their reading skills were at best limited. It was that ancient documents were mostly written in *scriptum continuum* — a continuous flow of letters without separation of words, sentences, paragraphs, and with little or no punctuation, and, verily, no chapters and verses at all. There were plenty of people who studied their religious traditions, but had minimal literacy. How did they do it?

First of all, they had teachers who taught them to listen intently, memorize what they were taught, and then recite it. Instead of notes on papyrus, they stored up things in their hearts, as the psalmist says. Being a disciple in such a culture meant listening first of all. In an oral culture it is understandable that Jesus said to his disciples, "Let those with two good ears, hear." Most eyes in antiquity could not read a document written in scriptum continuum. In addition to teachers or sages, and scribes who did most of the writing, there were also "readers," by which I mean lectors — people who could read such ancient documents, and were commissioned to do so. Let us consider a couple of examples from Scripture.

Some scholars, on the basis of the occasional reference to "readers" in the New Testament, have thought this signaled that Christians were some of the first to self-consciously be trying to produce "books," or even literature meant for reading. For example, sometimes Mark's Gospel has been called the first Christian book, in large part based on the reference in Mark 13:14 where we find the parenthetical remark, "let the reader understand," on the assumption that the "reader" in question is the audience. But let us examine this assumption for a moment.

Both in Mark 13:14 and in Revelation 1:3 the operative Greek words are *ho anaginoskon,* a clear reference to a single and singular reader, who in the Revelation 1:3 text is clearly distinguished from the audience who are dubbed the hearers (plural!) of John's rhetoric. As Mark Wilson suggested in a public lecture at Ephesus, this surely is likely to mean that the singular reader is in fact a lector of sorts, someone who will be reading John's apocalypse out loud to various hearers.[3] We know for a fact that John is addressing various churches in Asia Minor (see Revelation 2–3), so it is quite impossible to argue that the reference to "the reader" singular in Revelation 1:3 refers to the audience. It must refer to the rhetor or lector who will orally deliver this discourse to the audience of hearers.

I would suggest that we must draw the same conclusion about the parenthetical remark in Mark 13:14, which in turn means that not even Mark's Gospel should be viewed as a text, meant for private reading, much less the first real modern "text" or "book." Rather, Mark is reminding the lector, who will be orally delivering the Gospel in some or several venues near to the time when this "abomination" would be or was already arising, to help the audience understand the nature of what was happening when the temple in Jerusalem was being destroyed. Oral texts often include such reminders for the ones delivering the discourse in question.

The texts of the Bible were oral texts, which meant in the first instance that they were meant to be heard, being read by someone who was capable of doing so. The way education worked in such a setting is that listeners would memorize things that they heard and had repeated to them various times. Studying meant working

3. In a lecture delivered by him at a conference at Ephesus in May 2008, where we both spoke on the oral character of these New Testament texts.

The Rest of Life

with both a teacher and a lector if need be. But there was still more reason for study to be mainly oral and aural in antiquity, besides the literacy rate. The production of documents was a slow and costly procedure.

Papyrus was expensive, ink was expensive, hiring a scribe was expensive, and the process of writing a lengthy document — like, say, Hebrews — could take a considerable period of time. It would appear that most learning in a Jewish setting was done by rote memorization. This makes sense of various things we observe in the Gospels. For example, we never find mentioned any scribes sitting around taking notes when Jesus spoke. Why not? For one thing, most of the disciples may not have been able to afford papyrus, or to write. This did not make them illiterate. They could learn, and they could likely read to some extent.

The point, however, is that they learned, and they studied by listening and repeating what they heard. One of the more famous early Jewish sayings about teachers and their disciples goes like this: "To what shall we compare a true disciple?" "He is like a plastered cistern, never losing a single drop of the master's teaching." How was this possible? In some cases it was done simply by storing things up in one's heart and reciting it regularly with one's lips. It is interesting that the essence of "home-schooling" in antiquity is that a *paidagogos* might be employed, a literate slave, who not only walked the young student back and forth to his school, but helped him at home recite his lessons until he knew them by heart. It is this last point that should be stressed. Even in the home, study and education involved recitation of lessons or sayings or stories or laws, and memorization. And this brings me to a point in regard to our own pedagogical situation.

Maybe in an age where people don't want to read, but need to study God's Word to better understand God, it might be wise to consider going back to basic memorization and recitation methods as part of the overall pedagogy. Maybe we need to stop trying to entertain our congregations and students and go back to making sure they actually have learned at least the script of the Scriptures. Maybe a combination of using visual learning techniques and memorization could be the foundational building block to help more people begin to store up God's Word in their hearts. It's worth pondering and meditating on.

What is clear to me from Psalm 119 is the psalmist is quite sure that one of the things that keep him on the straight and narrow ethically is learning God's commandments. Yes, he also asks for extra help from God to keep his ways straight, but the clear message of the psalm is that the less well you know God's Word the more likely it is that you will or can justify misbehaving. And what does that tell us about where we are today in an age of widespread biblical illiteracy? It seems not to have occurred to us that there is a connection between that and the way we behave. It's not just that knowledge is power, and with knowledge comes accountability. It's that God's Word itself, when it lodges inside the human heart, is transformative — affecting our thoughts, attitudes, words, and deeds.

There is another side to this reality as well, as described in Hebrews 4:12-13: "For the word of God is alive and powerful. It is sharper than the sharpest two-edged sword, cutting between soul and spirit, between joint and marrow. It exposes our innermost thoughts and desires. Nothing in all creation is hidden from God. Everything is naked and exposed before his eyes, and he is the one to whom we are accountable." The author is not talking about the written-down word of God but rather the oral word of God proclaimed; nonetheless he is saying that when it gets inside a person it is like a searchlight that exposes our innermost thoughts and convicts and convinces us about what we have done wrong. Knowledge of God's Word and will leads to accountability to God for our thoughts and behavior. It is interesting how God's Word in this passage is basically equated with God's eyes searching out what is going on in our innermost being, or to use his other analogy, it is like a scalpel getting right to the source of the problem.

The other side of this coin, which is equally telling, is that while with knowledge comes more accountability, and indeed more convictability (God using his word to convict us when we go astray), on the other hand ignorance is not bliss, but it can be a mitigating factor when it comes to holding someone accountable for their sin. Consider, for example, Jesus' word from the cross about his tormentors: "Father, forgive them for they do not know what they are doing" (Luke 23:34), or the theme in the early chapters of Acts (Acts 1–5) where Peter says that the Jewish authorities handed Jesus over in ignorance, which proves to be a mitigating factor that allows Peter to offer them the opportunity to repent and believe the gospel. Or again consider Jesus' words in John 9:41 after the Pharisees have asked, "Are we blind too?" to which he replies, "If you were blind, you would not be guilty of sin, but now that you claim you can see, your guilt remains." Clearly with more knowledge comes more accountability, or in this case, if you claim "to see" you are held accountable whether you really see or not. Perhaps the lesson here is that a little knowledge, and claiming to know more than you do, is a dangerous thing when it comes to knowledge of God and his ways.

What is perhaps most interesting about the discussions in Hebrews and in Luke and John that we have just been reflecting on is that sin can be both theological and ethical, and the knowledge needed to help prevent one from sinning is both theological and ethical. But the even deeper issue is what one does with what one knows, and whether it transforms a hard heart, a heart of stone, into a heart that deeply desires and strives to know and please God, or not. The issue ultimately is spiritual transformation, and studying and knowing is seen as one of the keys to that happening. It is also seen as a key to continuing on the right path theologically and ethically, once one has begun down the right road.

If we conceive of the Christian life as an ongoing journey, then it becomes clear that since there are many possible roads to go down every day, it is not the case that one needs a GPS just to get on the right road in the first place. One needs that GPS device continually to keep one on the right road. Put another way, studying God's Word and drawing closer to God is continually essential to reaching the Kingdom goal and entering through the narrow gate. It is also essential to growing up and maturing in Christ as Hebrews 5–6 suggests, allowing one to make better judgments and better decisions in life about life's choices.

Moderns tend to think of education as one stage in life's journey, after which we go on to make a living. What the Bible says is that we are never finished gaining the knowledge of God and his will, and never cease to need to be better informed about which way to go on this day or tomorrow, or the day after that. Study of God's Word and will for the Christian is not a mere esoteric pursuit of knowledge; it is an essential means of growing in Christ, and going in the right direction towards all that we were meant to be, towards full conformity to Christ's image.

In Sum

This in turn brings us finally to an eschatological vision of study. Paul tells us in 1 Corinthians 13 that the day is coming where faith will become sight, and hopes will be realized, and we will know as we are known. While salvation is much more than just knowing, especially if by knowing we mean "knowing about" God (even the demons know the truth about God, but that truth has not transformed them), rather than having intimate personal experience of God, nevertheless, we are told that one day we will see God face to face, and know him as we are known. Some more fatalistic Christians when they have read this passage in 1 Corinthians 13 have concluded that we don't really need to do all this study and learning of God's Word now; it's just about our personal experiences of God, because, after all, if we just make it into eternity, then suddenly we will know as we are known. So what's the point of all this studying here and now?

The answer to this question is severalfold. Do we really want to hear Jesus say to us when we see him face to face, "It's a shame you didn't give me more to work with when you were serving me in the world, because you were too lazy to study diligently God's Word," or would you rather hear him say, "Well done, good and faithful servant, inherit the Kingdom"? Studying makes a Christian a more useful servant of the Lord here and now — a better witness, a better teacher, a better preacher, a better Bible study leader, a better youth worker. You get the picture.

The second reason to study now, and not just wait until we know everything at the eschaton, or in heaven (and by the way Revelation 6 suggests that in heaven even the martyrs still have questions like "How long, O Lord?"), is because as Psalm 119 stresses, all other things being equal the more one understands God's Word, the less one is likely to accidentally go astray, and perhaps as well the less likely one is to intentionally go astray. Knowledge of God's Word in the heart is not an absolute protection against wandering thoughts or aberrant behavior, but, as Hebrews says, it is God's searchlight that can convict and convince us of things. Remember the story of the young college girl who came to see Fred Craddock at the beginning of this discussion? Finally, there is this: Do we want to please God? If it is our deepest desire to please God, then when God's Word tells us that we need to commit ourselves to diligent study, learning, memorization of God's Word, why would we take those sorts of commandments casually, as if it were not that important?

I once had a student who came up to me very frustrated after a New Testament Intro class. He said, "I don't know why I need to learn all this stuff about history and archaeology and literary stuff, when I can just get up into the pulpit and the Spirit will give me utterance." My response was, "Yes, you can do that, but it is a shame you are not giving the Holy Spirit more to work with." I would here add, it was a shame he was not more willing to listen to all the exhortations about studying in the Bible and thus did not realize this was a good way to please God. If the great commandment is to love God with all our hearts and *all our minds,* loving God with all our minds necessarily involves studying diligently God's Word throughout our lives so that we may see him more clearly, love him more dearly, and follow him more nearly day by day. That way, when we do see God face to face, when faith becomes full knowledge, it will simply be the completion of a journey we have been on for a long time — a long obedience in the same direction, as Eugene Peterson has called it. It will not be a big surprise with a lot of reprimands at the end. Jesus did not die on the cross so that we might become lazy about the pursuit of the knowledge of God, thinking we have salvation already in the bag. He did not come and teach us the Sermon on the Mount so that we could then make false dichotomies between law and grace and between faith and obedience and between faith and knowledge, as if only grace and only faith mattered. That's not a version of the gospel; that's a perversion of the gospel. So let us listen to the words of the psalmist once more:

"Blessed are those who keep God's statutes and seek him with all their heart — they do no wrong, but follow his ways" (Ps. 119:2). He then asks, "How can a young person keep their ways pure?" And he answers, "By living according to your word" (Ps. 119:9). This is why immediately afterwards he says, "I have hidden your word in my heart, that I might not sin against you." Study, learning, memorizing, hiding the word in one's heart, is allowing God's searchlight into your innermost being. It is a key to avoiding sin, a means of drawing closer to God, a way of pleasing God and showing that you love him, and a preparation for seeing God face to face and *being able to recognize the Lord when you finally see him.* Thinking about study in the light of Kingdom come makes it clear that we study now to find ourselves approved then. But it also reminds us that if we want power and authority in our lives and in our ministries, there is no greater source of this than a deep and abiding knowledge of God and of his Word. And this, quite frankly, requires a pilgrimage involving lifelong learning.

CHAPTER FIVE

Sex and the City of God

Sex is the most wonderful thing on this earth, as long as God is in it. When the Devil gets in it, it's the most terrible thing on this earth.

Billy Graham, Just as I Am

It was a decidedly mixed message. My junior high youth-group leader was doing his best to explain to us all a Christian perspective on sex, but he was struggling. Perhaps the struggle was that he was trying to say two contradictory things at once. On the one hand he wanted to say that sex is a good gift from God. On the other hand, the real message I kept hearing was, "Sex is dirty; save it for the one you really love." If that is not a mixed message, I don't know what is.

It seems the church has too often been guilty of misreading what the Bible says about sex. And actually the Bible has plenty to say about it. The church has even been embarrassed by a whole book of the Old Testament — the Song of Songs, and turned it into an allegory of Christ as the bridegroom and the church as the bride. This artful dodge is unfortunately not in any way a legitimate interpretation of that beautiful poem. No, the Song of Songs is a moderately steamy love poem about a royal ruler and his love for his girl. If this embarrasses us, then it tells us that we are out of line with the biblical view of sex.

But there is a difference, as we shall see, between something God gave us for our earthly good, like sexual intercourse and marriage, and something that is an eternal good and will continue to be a part of life when the Kingdom comes in eternity. There are timely goods, and there are timeless goods, and sexual intercourse is one of the former. That doesn't in any way diminish the importance of sex and its goodness as part of life in this world. But it does put it in perspective. Sex is not the be-all and end-all of existence. Life in the Kingdom will not involve marrying, giving in marriage, or sex. We won't need any of that. We will have union and communion and bliss and joy and ecstasy between ourselves and God and between ourselves and all other Kingdom dwellers. In a sense it will be like being married to everyone, or better said, all of us being part of the family that is married to the bridegroom — Christ. We will say much more about this at the end of this chapter. There are important things to say before we get to that discussion.

Sex God

There have been many books written about Christians and sex over the years, and the one that has gotten the most attention in the last few years is Rob Bell's *Sex God* (2007). A good place then for us to enter the current discussion is by interacting with this book in some depth.

The first thing we need to make clear about the title *Sex God* is that Bell is not talking about some sort of ancient Near East fertility deity like Baal or Astarte. He is talking about the connection between sexuality and spirituality and how the former figures forth the latter in various ways. It is a profound subject, and one well worth pursuing. My own observation would be that there is a fine line between a person's spirituality and their sexuality, and some-times these two things get confused and fused. A person who is pas-sionate in the way of *eros* is also prone to be passionate in the way of *agape;* hence some of the cautionary words in the Bible about sex. When you get people revved up about love of God *and neighbor,* it is understandable they might also get revved up about sex.

The preface to Bell's book lays out the groundwork for what follows, and the "this is that" principle. Bell is able to point to things like piles of standing stones, or old trophies, or the like, which have little worth or significance in themselves except for what they remind us of, what they point us to. While Bell in no way wants to trivialize the reality or goodness of human sexuality (to the contrary, this book does the opposite), what he does want to say is that "sex" points to something much bigger, larger, and spiritual about human beings and reality. For one thing, it points to the fact that we are created in the image of a creative and lively God. Indeed, we are created male and female for each other, which is to say, we were created for bonding between genders, and one-flesh unions, among other things. The image itself is not the gen-der distinction — but the two things are related.

The first chapter, titled "God Wears Lipstick," is powerful in various ways, in that Bell talks about the factors that reduce hu-man beings to subhuman things, and alternately the things that humanize us. He makes the strong point of how our culture en-courages us to objectify women, treating sexual persons as sex ob-jects. Of course this sort of reductionism would seldom happen if fallen males did not lust after women's body parts. It has gotten so bad that you can even see it in the way men look at women. They tend to look at their breasts first and then their faces, thinking of what they want before thinking of who they want. When another person is used as a means to an end, a means to scratch your own selfish itch, then we are dealing with lust and not love. And our culture can't easily distinguish the two. Lots of times we hear peo-ple say "we're in love," but in fact what is meant is "we're in heat."

Unlike Gaia theologians, or even some Wicca folks, Bell rightly distinguishes between being made in God's image (an asexual thing) and being made male and female. God is not a great white male in the sky. Indeed Jesus tells us in John 4 that God is spirit — not The Spirit, but spirit. That is, God is a nonmaterial being, and since genders require an embodied existence, we could hardly be "male and female" in the image of God, if God has no gender in his divine essence. It is true that God the Son took on a human nature at one juncture, but even *his* divine essence is not gendered. God, the biblical God, in the divine essence is not male or female.[1]

Bell tells a compelling story about a woman during World War II in Bergen-Belsen prison. When one is stripped of all possessions and all dignity as well, even little scraps of normal life can help keep one human. And so for this woman something as simple as lipstick made her feel human and a person of worth all over again. We need those things that protect us from the forces that strip us of our humanity in this world — and war absolutely does that. But oddly enough, something else that strips us of our humanity is the cheapening of something as sacred as sex. You might think that the more sex of any sort, the more we are being truly human. But in fact if you talk to a prostitute she will tell you the opposite. She has become numb; a sacrament has been defiled. More sex has not made her more truly human; it has stripped her of her true humanity and dignity.

Chapter 2, "Sexy on the Inside," starts with the interesting observation that many people who are not religious nonetheless have this sense that things in the world are not as they are intended to be and that we are supposed to be connected to each other and the world and not treat each other poorly. This is true enough, and I have encountered this as well. I would put it down

1. Rob Bell, *Sex God: Exploring the Endless Connections Between Sexuality and Spirituality* (Grand Rapids: Zondervan, 2007), p. 24.

to the fact that even people who are oblivious to God are still created in God's image and occasionally have *Aha* moments where these kinds of insights dawn on them. This chapter is largely about our sense of disconnection with the earth and with each other and how it goes back to the story of Adam and Eve, where the curse involves this disconnect between us and the earth, and between man and woman.

Bell offers the interesting etymology for the word "sex" from *secare* — the Latin for "cut off" (from which we get *sect, bisect, sectarian,* etc.). In fact, sicarri were the dagger men, the hit men among the early Jewish zealots who cut off other people's lives. He then says, "our sexuality is our awareness of how profoundly we're severed and cut off and disconnected. Second, our sexuality is all of the ways we go about trying to reconnect."[2]

Bell deals with the Genesis idea that self-awareness in the case of Adam involved a sense of being cut off from God, and being focused on self. He actually wants to define sexuality in a broad way — it's all the ways we try to connect with each other, with God, even with the earth. In my view this is too broad a definition of sexuality. Our desire for oneness with God is not really a sexual desire. And indeed the sense of oneness with creation, with the earth, such as we see in Psalm 8 is not really a sense of sexuality as it is usually defined. But it is true that our sexuality is part of the larger tactile package of aspects of human nature that prompt and impel us towards connection with the "Other." I think Bell is confusing or fusing the deep sense of intimacy and oneness with some "other" person or thing, with the concept of sexuality. Intimacy and communion are broader categories than sexuality, actually.

He is right, however, that there can be lots of physical interacting, including intercourse, with little or no real connection made. But wait a moment — Paul in 1 Corinthians 5–6 says that even sex with a prostitute involves becoming one flesh with her,

2. Bell, *Sex God,* p. 40.

and by that Paul means something sexual but also something spiritual is involved such that it interferes with the one spirit union you have with Jesus. I take Bell's point, however, that having sex with someone you are not married to and trust and committed to can leave you alone and lonely and unfulfilled.

I like the definition of "feeling sexy" as feeling good to be in your own skin, your own body shape, etc. I do not agree that we must first be at peace with who we are, in order to be connected with God. This gets the cart before the horse. In fact, I think when God reconciles himself to us, redeems us, that's when we just begin to understand who and whose we are and to be at peace with who we are. It is true that if we are unwilling to change our dysfunctionality and our unhealthy images of self we will never fully benefit from our relationship with the Lord, never fully be whole or healed. But there are many Christians who have been deeply uncomfortable in their own skin, and not at peace with who they are, and yet have had profound relationships with God.

In chapter 3, "Angels and Animals," Bell gets down to brass tacks, or better said, basic instincts. He carefully deconstructs the myths that (1) we are just the sum of our urges or desires; (2) that abstinence is somehow a limitation of our freedom or even a way of being dishonest with ourselves; (3) that we are simply animals and that therefore we could hardly expect not to act like animals. I especially like the way he draws a contrast between lions in heat (who are clearly not thinking "Do we have a meaningful relationship?" or "Can I trust you?" or "Why do you say I only want you for your body?") and human beings. I quite agree that much of modernity falsely assumes that people cannot transcend their basic instincts, and if they repress them they will be unfulfilled and indeed unhealthy people. Bell also deals with the difficulties of living in a culture where purity and chastity are ridiculed.

He then turns around and deals with the angel instinct, the mindset that fails to acknowledge our physical and sexual nature and the way it influences our thinking and behavior, or even fails to acknowledge that our sexuality is central to what makes us human.[3] I agree with him on this, and his basic argument is that we have to live in tension between the animal and angel instinct. However, there are a few flies in the ointment here.

Bell is right that angels are by nature spirits. However, early Jewish tradition believed they could be male or female, and indeed that they could even have sex. For example, Genesis 6:1-4 was traditionally read as the story about angels (called "sons of god" here and in some other places as well) mating with human women, producing a hideous hybrid between the two sorts of beings. It is precisely this gross violation of the creation order that prompts the flood, according to Genesis 6. Furthermore, Jesus himself famously said that "we will be like the angels in heaven, neither marrying nor giving in marriage." This refers to the act of marrying, not to having sex per se, though the two are connected. Jesus' point is that we will not be starting any new marriage relationships in the next life at all. In this regard we will be like the angels, not sexless but rather unmarried. There are no married angels, according to the Jewish tradition.

There is this further deficiency in Bell's discussion about being angels. He says that if we don't express our sexuality, if we just stuff our sexual feelings, then we are repressed. This is a traditional modern psychological view of the matter. But what about the person called by God to remain a single person? He or she still has sexual feelings. While he may talk about them, he is not supposed to act in a sexual manner. Is that repression or restraining one's self in a healthy way by the grace of God? Paul's advice in 1 Corinthians 7 comes to mind here.

Paul counsels an engaged couple to remain as they are, keeping his virgin as a virgin, but if he can't restrain himself he should go ahead and marry. Better to marry than to burn with passion. But clearly Paul believes that persons like himself can and do re-

3. Bell, *Sex God*, p. 54.

strain themselves, that there is a place for being single and not sexually active, though it requires God's grace to remain chaste, and he would hardly call this sexual repression. Nor, I think, would Jesus. I do, however, very much like the way Bell's chapter ends — namely with the remark that we are always in the process of creating order out of chaos. The creation process is still an ongoing thing, and we have something to contribute to it.

Chapter 4 is provocatively titled "Leather, Whips, and Fruit," and deals with the sordid topic of lust, which, as Bell says, promises what it cannot deliver. One of Bell's theses here is that lust comes from a deep sense of dissatisfaction with one's life or situation. He contrasts it with gratitude. There is something to this. It would have helped to distinguish between lust and desire. Lust is always sinful; desire is not necessarily so.

In the middle of a useful discussion Bell tells us that the word *epithumia* means "in the mind." Actually it does not. It means "in fury" or "in rage" (i.e., enraged) and refers to deep feelings, not deep thoughts. I do however like his definition of freedom — it isn't being able to have what we crave, but rather being able to go without what we crave and be fine with it.[4] The basic advice is to channel our desires, our energies, into positive and good things. This is very common advice indeed, but wise nonetheless. For example, being obsessive-compulsive can be a bane or a blessing. A person who channels it in the right direction can get a lot done, done well, in order, and on time. But channeled in the wrong way it can lead to greed, the need to have all of this set of books, or all of Madonna's CDs, or the like. Life is not about toning down our energies, but in fact about letting our desires be absorbed into a higher and greater desire, enterprise, opportunity.

Chapter 5 is an exposition on love, and there is a very effective spinning out of the story of Song of Songs, a poem that proclaims the goodness of sexual desire and expression in the right context.

4. Bell, *Sex God*, p. 75.

The Rest of Life

Happily, Bell doesn't turn this story into an allegory about Christ and the church. Bell also explores the love of God for us, focusing on how God grieves, has heartaches, and is pained — and as it says in Genesis 6, regrets having made humans. One of the more helpful and profound insights is that love is a giving away of power, a becoming vulnerable.[5] Is that true of God as well? Bell says yes — look at Jesus. He adds: "Love is giving up control. It's surrendering the desire to control the other person. The two — love and controlling power over the other person — are mutually exclusive. If we are serious about loving someone, we have to surrender all the desires within us to manipulate the relationship."[6]

There are two very striking implications to this: (1) If what Bell says is true, then love is never a power move, never irresistible, even when we are talking about God. That pretty much rules out certain Calvinistic views of love and God right there. Love does not demand its own way, says Paul (1 Cor. 13), and Jesus shows us this is the way God loves us. (2) This definition of love also means that we are to sacrifice and put the other person first in our marriages. My wife is so much better at this than I am, I must confess. But this definition of love rules out the same old patriarchal stuff.

When Christian love appears on the scene, it's all about mutual submission, as Ephesians 5:21 says, mutual sacrifice and service. We need to keep in mind that Paul in the household codes is trying to push an existing patriarchal situation, a de facto way of life, in a more Christian direction. We get glimmerings of where it's all going in places like Ephesians 5:21, where we see the highest and best way the relationship can work. What Paul believes is that the leaven of the gospel is being put into the Christian community and its relationships so that things will move away from the fallen patriarchal world order to a more egalitarian one.

Bell brings out quite well how love is risky for God as well, be-

5. Bell, *Sex God*, p. 98.
6. Bell, *Sex God*, p. 98.

cause we may respond negatively. He stresses that the death of Jesus reflects a condemnation of the domination systems that oppress people. In this Bell sounds a bit like John Dominic Crossan, but I think he is at least partly right. We have a catchy statement at the end of the chapter: "God can do anything — that's what makes God, God. But God can't do everything. God can't make us love him — that's our choice."[7]

In fact, God could have set up the whole system differently and *made* us respond positively to him, but Bell's point seems to be that that response, however little it seemed coerced, would not be love. Love can neither be predetermined nor coerced. I agree. And it is not an accident that the New Testament never says God is power (the noun) though it does say God is almighty (the adjective). On the other hand it absolutely does say that God is love. The essence of who God is, is love. This is why Jesus is the clearest, highest, most effective, and most powerful revelation of the divine nature. God has deliberately limited himself in order to take on flesh, take on suffering, take on death in the person of Jesus, and be a love letter to humanity. I am reminded of the powerful poem by Geoffrey Studdert-Kennedy, "The Sorrow of God," which in essence says that God suffers when we suffer. We see this in Jesus' words to Saul on the Damascus road: "Saul, why do you persecute me?" We see it in Jesus' words, "inasmuch as you have done it unto the least of these." God does not merely empathize with us; he knows our pain and suffers with us in some mysterious way.

Chapter 6, "Worth Dying For," may be the best chapter in any of Bell's books. He understands very well the difficulties in discussing the submission passages, and he handles it like a pro. He rightly stresses that mutual submission is what Ephesians 5:21 is calling all Christians to in relationship to each other, and a particular illustration of that is found in the relationship of Christian wife and husband. The husband indeed is called the head, but the

7. Bell, *Sex God*, p. 109.

job descriptor for headship is to take the lead in serving, sacrificing, and loving, just as Christ did. If this is not a form of self-emptying and submitting, I don't know what it is. Bell adds: "The husband's waiting for his wife to submit is actually a failure to lead. . . . If he really thinks he is the head, then he would surrender his desires and wants and plans. He would die to his need to be in control and do whatever it takes to serve her. . . . He would die to himself so that she could live."[8] Exactly so. It's time we renounced the non-Christian nonsense about unilateral submission of women to men in the church, in marriage, in ministry, in general. Bell then adds, "In marriage, you're talking about power and control only when something central to the whole relationship has fallen apart."[9] Yes, that's right, and perhaps the two persons have never come to fully give themselves, fully trust each other yet, and so they are still negotiating the landscape and boundaries of the relationship. Perhaps one or the other or both of them are insecure and afraid the relationship is getting out of their control — hence the power move.

I like Bell's exposition of 1 Corinthians 7 as well — the bodies of husband and wife belong to each other, not to themselves. Amen to that, and this means that "conjugal rights" are more like "conjugal obligations" — we are called to freely give ourselves up to the other, not demand our right to the other's body, our right to sex on demand. True lovers give up their rights, and abandon themselves in trying to please the other — never demanding anything. Bell answers the question of who has the authority in this relationship by saying "yes," they both have authority over each other's body. In Paul's world this would have clashed with the sexual double standard that meant wives needed to stay chaste while husbands were allowed to visit the prostitutes.

The exposition of *agape* love is helpful as well. *Agape* is un-

8. Bell, *Sex God,* p. 117.
9. Bell, *Sex God,* p. 119.

conditional love, not love that is bestowed only when someone is worthy. "Agape loves in such a way that it makes them beautiful."[10] Just so; that's what God's love does. "People are loved into their futures," their future best selves.[11] Bell tells women, "You don't need to use your body to get what you need. It's a cop-out for not being a certain kind of woman — a woman of dignity and honor."[12]

Bell then talks about how women trade sex for validation, affection, and an affirmation that they are worth something. "Sex becomes a search. A search for something they're missing. A quest for the unconditional embrace. And so they go from relationship to relationship, looking for what they already have. . . . But sex is not the search for something missing. It's the expression of something that's been found. It's designed to be the overflow, the culmination of something that a man and woman have found in each other. . . . It's a celebration of this living breathing thing that's happening between the two of them."[13] Bell goes on to add a strong paragraph on where our worth comes from. It comes from being created in God's image, being loved by God unconditionally. It does not come from your body, your mind, your work, what you produce or put out. It doesn't come from whether you have a spouse or a girlfriend or boyfriend or whether people notice you, or whether you are famous. Your great worth comes from your Creator.

Chapter 7, "Under the Chuppah," is about having enough sense to keep various things in your married life between the two of you. A *Chuppah* is a canopy under which the bride and groom, and no one else, stand in a Jewish wedding. Only they are under the canopy of God's eye of protection for that particular relationship, and there are things in the relationship that should be be-

10. Bell, *Sex God*, p. 120.
11. Bell, *Sex God*, p. 121.
12. Bell, *Sex God*, p. 122.
13. Bell, *Sex God*, p. 123.

tween them and God, and no one else. There is a useful discussion in this chapter of the Old Testament material, where God's relationship to his people is described as being like the relationship of husband and wife — actually the latter is modeled on the former to some extent. The analogy in Hosea between God and his people and husband and wife is especially well developed. It is interesting how Bell sees the ten commandments as like the *ketubah,* the wedding contract. Accepting the ten commandments is agreeing to love no one but God the spouse alone, and agreeing to the other natural implications of this commitment, expressed in the other stipulations. The problem with this analogy is that a marriage covenant and its stipulations are different from a covenant between a king and his vassals, and in fact the Old Testament covenants are more like those ancient Near East treaties than like marriage contracts.

Bell tells us that, in Jewish marriage law, a couple is not married until they have sex. He talks about the wedding canopy being put up over the marriage bed; the couple have sex while the guests wait outside (!), and then they come out and have the wedding party now that they are fully married. The problem with this analysis (which is only partially right) is that the marriage contract, which was decided on well before the marriage, was binding long before the consummation of the union.[14] This is why, in Matthew, Joseph had thought to "divorce" Mary before they had come together. One can say that the contracting is the beginning of the marriage, not merely an engagement period with no legal force, and the consummation is the conclusion of the act of marrying someone. Unlike our way of doing it, Jewish marriage takes a long while — not twenty minutes in a chapel.

In this chapter we also discover that Bell has a healthy sense of progressive revelation. He talks about how in Jewish law, a man who has sex with a woman is then required to marry and take care

14. Bell, *Sex God,* pp. 134-35.

of her, which is light-years ahead of the practices in the ancient Near East where she is permanently shamed by such an act and simply discarded and the man has no obligation to her. As he says, this is a higher view of what sex creates — a one-flesh union, not a lower one. Then in the New Testament we go a big step further, in which men are commanded to lay down their lives for their wives and engage in mutuality of sacrifice and submission.[15]

The exclusiveness of the relationship of marriage is important. The giving of one's self totally to another person is gripping in a wedding service — it is the exclusivity of it that makes it special and powerful. Bell adds that we must guard this, because when we have given it away to someone else, we no longer have it, and no longer share that unique kind of sharing meant for husband and wife. Bell stresses that when you take sex outside of marriage you cheapen it; all you are left with is mechanics, not love. Sex taken out of its God-intended context loses its mystery and specialness. It leaves nothing to the imagination.

What does it mean to have a one-flesh union? Bell focuses on the Hebrew word *echad,* which means "one." This word refers to a oneness that is made up of more than one member — it is thus applied to the one-flesh union of husband and wife, but also it is the word for "one" in the Shema, in reference to the divine nature. From this he infers that God's oneness is complex, made up of several factors, parts, members united as one. I agree with this analysis.

And this is where we finally get to the punch line as to why this book is called *Sex God* — because the oneness experienced in sex points beyond itself to the oneness that exists in God. Our one-flesh union refers to, alludes to, symbolizes, foreshadows that. Bell sees marriage as a picture of the oneness we all seek and yearn for with each other as well. His exposition on the Genesis phrase from the creation story ("they were naked and felt no shame") is

15. Bell, *Sex God,* pp. 136-37.

useful — complete acceptance as the other is, without embarrassment on either side and without much self-consciousness. He stresses that nakedness of body should only be shared with one who shares nakedness of soul with you. Being naked means peeling back the layers and letting down the defenses of body and soul — those two things should be done together, in harmony. If you share your body but not your soul it's like having and holding and sharing the wineskins but not the wine.

The last chapter, "Whoopee Forever," rounds out the discussion. Bell points to the places in the teaching of Jesus and Paul where the goodness of remaining single is stressed, and the temporary nature of human marriage is also stressed. Marriage is indeed a this-world institution meant for our earthly and temporal and temporary good — not something eternal. Marriage brings hope, and oneness, and continuation of the race in this world, but in the next one there will be no new acts of marrying. As I have said, in a sense it will be like we are all married to each other in the Kingdom, the communion or koinonia will be so grand.

Bell asks: "If sex is about connection, what happens when everybody is connected with everybody else?"[16] What happens at the eschaton when all are one in God's presence? Bell asks if sex and its moments of ecstasy are a picture of heaven or the bliss in the new creation. While some have compared it to the mystical ascent called the beatific vision of God, Bell is comparing it to our eschatological experience of God in due course. Good sex and marriage are a picture of heaven on earth — sort of like what Jesus describes as preparing for his disciples in John 14:2-4. The epilogue of the book finishes with a reminder about relationships that fail, and the forgiveness and healing that are possible thereafter — a realistic pastoral note.

This book is in so many ways an important book in any discussion today of sex and Christians. And it is a good thing that

16. Bell, *Sex God*, p. 167.

Bell rightly analyzes the whole issue in the light of eternity, from a Kingdom come and Kingdom coming perspective, which frees us up from either turning sex or marriage into an idol, or trivializing and secularizing it into something of little importance. But there is much more to say, so let's start with Paul — which inevitably seems to be the bone of contention in so many discussions.

Was Paul a Prude?

In his recent discussion about sex and intimacy, my friend and colleague Dr. James Howell has this to say on the matter:

> God must blush, and grieve. The world is good — and Genesis goes to great lengths to clarify that sex in particular is perhaps God's most extravagant gift — and not merely sexual activity, but our bodies, our identities. The world is good; God didn't create us as riddled with angst, guilt, and reckless desire. Evil is a perversion of the good, a twisting of the beautiful.
>
> In Genesis, God's first command to humanity is to "be fruitful and multiply"; far from being *un*spiritual, sex is profoundly spiritual: physical intimacy, and our stewardship of the body, is a primal way we enact our faith, and follow Christ in the real world. Not surprisingly, then, idolatry, the worship of false gods, almost always has a sexual connotation in the Bible. Russ Reno explains that the idolater has much in common with the adulterer — who wants sexual union but not children. "The idolater is like a man who visits prostitutes; he wants the pleasure without the responsibility — just as the idolater wants to worship but reserve the power to live as he pleases." Just as a man who has an illicit relationship hopes she will keep quiet, so the idolater is not all that disappointed if his god is silent — for to hear from God would be rather inconvenient.
>
> Genesis rather wonderfully tells us that Adam and Eve

were unclothed, but also unashamed. Of course, the very mention of their lack of shame is a dark foreshadowing of the day when there *will* be shame, when their lost innocence will be the ruin of their joy, faith and sense of goodness. It is intriguing to consider the loss of shame in modern culture. Teens and even children are far from ready emotionally to cope with what they are exposed to through the media. Neil Postman, in his brilliant *The Disappearance of Childhood*, suggests we have lost shame — good shame: "Without a well-developed idea of shame, childhood cannot exist. Children need to be sheltered from adult secrets, particularly sexual secrets. If we turn over to children a vast store of powerful adult material, childhood cannot survive. By definition adulthood means mysteries solved and secrets uncovered. If from the start the children know the mysteries and the secrets, how shall we tell them apart from anyone else?"

Genesis 3 calls us to the highest delight in the gift of sexuality, which requires a sense of beauty but also shame, a careful attentiveness to the distinction between beauty and the merely carnal, responsibility and irresponsibility.[17]

I think that Howell is absolutely right about all this. The question is — did Paul the Pharisee somehow forget or repudiate all he learned about the above topics and the real meaning of Genesis 1–3 when he became a Christian? Was Paul a prude, or even an ascetic? Unfortunately that is the way Paul, and in particular 1 Corinthians 7, has been read at various points in Christian history, even today by some. We need to revisit 1 Corinthians 7 in some detail and sort out whether Paul himself was the cause of later Christian asceticism and all sorts of deficient views of sex.

The structure of 1 Corinthians 7 may be broken down as follows:

17. James Howell in a blog post to his congregation Myers Park UMC in Charlotte, North Carolina. Posted and accessed June 26, 2011.

1. General discussion of marriage and conjugal rights (vv. 1-7)
2. Advice to widowers and widows (vv. 8-9)
3. Advice to married couples about separation and divorce (vv. 10-11)
4. Advice to those married to non-Christian spouses (vv. 12-16)
5. Illustrations of the principle "remain as you are" [in Christ] (vv. 17-24)[18]
6. Advice to those considering engagement and those already engaged (vv. 25-38)
7. Reiteration of advice and commands given to women in verses 8-11, with an additional comment on women's right to remarry (vv. 39-40).[19]

The first and in some ways most important thing to say to aid a proper contextual reading of this whole chapter is that Paul is responding to questions from the Corinthians here, and it is absolutely vital to distinguish their questions from Paul's answers. There were both ascetical and libertine factions in the Corinthian church, and Paul chooses not to address them directly, but he does quote the views of the ascetics at the outset of this argument. The argument begins, "Now concerning the things about which you wrote me: 'It is good for a man not to touch a woman.'" *This last sentence is not Paul's view, it is a quotation of someone who wrote to him who had ascetical views.* And Paul, as we shall see, will go on to say something quite the contrary to this — he will say that except for a time of prayer, a husband and wife should not refrain from conjugal relationships for any significant period of time. The fa-

---

18. Thanks to Scott Bartchy for urging me to stress that what Paul is saying here is: we should all remain as we are in Christ, whatever changes to our circumstances may happen. In other words, this is not at all a "stay in your station or social condition" argument.

19. The following discussion can be found in a much fuller form in Witherington, *Conflict and Community in Corinth: A Socio-Rhetorical Commentary on 1 and 2 Corinthians* (Grand Rapids: Eerdmans, 1995), pp. 173-85.

The Rest of Life

mous Pauline concession is not "conceding" that married couples should have sex. No, the concession is time apart from sex for prayer! Let's consider this passage in more detail.

Let's first be clear that Paul, because he is now apostle to the Gentiles and has much to do, prefers the single state to the married state, as it gives him more freedom to pursue the calling on his life. There is nothing particularly ascetical about his preference for singleness. And indeed it is likely that he is either a widower or a formerly married man, because Jewish males got married in their teens, and Paul was converted to Christianity only after he was well past that age. He had been a zealous Pharisee for some time before he had his U-turn on Damascus Road. The Pharisees were not advocates of celibacy for anyone who was able bodied, so far as we can tell. Both 1 Thessalonians 4:1-8 and 1 Corinthians 7:14 must count against any suggestion that Paul was ascetical by nature, or a prude, or somehow had a problem with sexual relationships in general.

The initial quote from the ascetical Corinthians says, "It is good for a man not to touch a woman," and "touch" here is definitely a Greek euphemism for "have sexual relationships with" (see Plutarch, *Pompey* 2.3; Aristotle, *Politics* 7.14.12; Josephus, *Jewish Antiquities* 1.163). Paul would obviously agree that there were various contexts in which such a thing was not merely inappropriate but immoral. But in the context of a heterosexual monogamous relationship, Paul views sexual intercourse as a good thing that should be engaged in regularly.

There are indeed some really remarkable aspects to the argument in 1 Corinthians 7, one of which is the notion that the husband's body belongs exclusively to the wife, and vice versa. In that patriarchal setting, while it would be a commonplace to say the wife must only share her body with the husband, placing the same stricture on the husband would be considered shocking, not least because all such marriages in Corinth were arranged marriages, set up mostly by parents, normally for children still in the home in their teens, and set up in the first place as property- and status-enhancing transactions, not love matches. In such a setting, in Greco-Roman relationships it was often taken for granted that the husband might well visit prostitutes or female "companions" to satisfy some of his sexual needs, especially when the family wanted no more children. Few Romans could have conceived of arguing that the husband's body belongs to the wife! It needs to be borne in mind that Paul's own eschatological views also condition his remarks here, as he will go on to urge that even married persons live with a certain sense of the contingency of their relationship — live "as if not" in light of the eschatological situation.

One of the repeated themes in this chapter is sexual passion, and the advice given is self-control (vv. 2, 5, 9, 36, 37). The fact that, contrary to usual precedent, Paul addresses women first in verses 4, 10, 11, 16, and 39 suggests that some of the Corinthian women Christians were particularly concerned about sex, engagement, marriage, divorce, and separation. I would suggest that since Paul is solving problems here, the fact that he focuses on passion and self-control probably reflects more on the problems in Corinth than on Paul's own views of marriage's purpose.

Indeed, the material in Colossians 3–4 and Ephesians 5–6 strongly suggests that Paul has a very positive and theologically grounded view of Christian marriage. We should not read 1 Corinthians 7 in isolation from what Paul says on this and related matters elsewhere. Even if we only concentrated on what is said in 1 Corinthians 7, it has to be stressed that Paul tells Christian women thinking about leaving their pagan spouses that they need not do so for fear of being made unclean through sexual contact or even general contact with their spouses. Indeed, says Paul, the Christian spouse "sanctifies" or "makes clean" the un-Christian one, and the progeny from such a union is "holy."

This view makes perfectly clear that (1) Paul does not see sex in the context of marriage as defiling in any way, even if one's partner is a pagan; and (2) in quite the opposite direction, Paul believes the Christian mate has a sanctifying effect on the non-Christian, and even on their conjugal relationships. Thus his word is that there is no "holiness" reason for the Christian spouse to depart from his or her mate, though he allows it if the pagan spouse is pursuing divorce. All of this paints a very different picture than the notion that Paul was either a sexual ascetic or a prude. In fact, Paul was no kind of ascetic at all. He was simply a man gifted to remain single for the Kingdom and true to his calling to be the pioneer apostle to the Gentiles.

One of the more important conclusions one must draw from a close reading of 1 Corinthians 7 has to do with Paul's use of the term *charisma* or grace gift. Paul will say that being single in Christ, and being married in the Lord, are both "grace gifts" from God. While this may seem rather conventional to our ears, in fact it is a radical teaching to suggest that singleness of any sort is a divine gift. It is an idea that had radical consequences, as well, for it meant that women, as well as men, no longer had to think purely in terms of the roles they might have in the physical family. They had a choice about such matters. This actually opened the door for women especially to play nontraditional roles in the service of the gospel and led to such famous second-century tales as the one told in "The Acts of Paul and Thecla," a story about how Paul and a woman named Thecla both did apostolic ministry in the province of Asia, including proclaiming God's word. This fact was enshrined in a cave above ancient Ephesus, where the two are painted on a wall of the cave where Christian worship took place.

Here I would stress that Paul is indeed saying that without God's enabling and gracing, a person cannot be properly single or properly married. It requires grace to live in either condition in a Christian way. Put another way, Paul is also suggesting that some people are simply not cut out for marriage; God has not given them that gift. In Paul's own case, however, he is saying that whatever may have been true in his former life as a Pharisee, now God has gifted him to remain single for the sake of the Kingdom, something Jesus himself talked about and exhibited in his own life (Matt. 19:10-12). To one and all, Paul stresses that the form of the world is already passing away because the Christ event has already happened, and therefore the priorities of the Kingdom relativize all other priorities in life for the Christian.

Here it will be useful to interact with the important work of Scott Bartchy, correcting Luther and his successors about the way 1 Corinthians 7:20-21 has been read, and indeed correcting mistakes in our basic lexicons along the way! First of all, the proper translation of 1 Corinthians 7:20-21 is as follows: "Each of you should remain in the calling [in Christ] by which you were called. Were you a slave when you were called? Don't worry about it. But if, indeed, you are able to become free, by all means live [as a freedman/freedwoman] according to God's calling."[20] The issue here in the first place has to do with the translation of a noun, *klesis,* which derives from the verb *kaleo,* which means to call. The problem began when Luther insisted on translating *klesis* with the German word *Beruf* ("occupation"/"status") instead of the correct German term *Ruf* ("call"/"summons"). This mistake was picked up first in the German lexicons, despite notable protests, and more recently in editions of the Bauer-Arndt-Gingrich-Danker lexicon, despite all the evidence to the contrary.[21] Luther, it must be said, appears to have been influenced by Augustine in this as well as in many other things. It was Augustine who first thought Paul was justifying slavery in this text. But Augustine was quite wrong.

As Bartchy makes clear, the following conclusions are warranted in regard to 1 Corinthians 7: (1) Paul is not baptizing the existing patriarchal and domination system status quo in 1 Corinthi-

20. Scott Bartchy has kindly given me a copy of the recent paper in which he persuasively argues his case — the first, titled "Paul Did Not Teach 'stay in slavery': The Mistranslation of *klesis* in 1 Cor. 7:20-21," was presented at the national SBL meeting in 2008.

21. Frederick Danker deserves the major credit for the most recent English edition update of BAGD.

ans 7. Paul clearly rejects the notions that followers of Christ are locked into a marriage with a nonbeliever, rejects the notion that entering a new marriage relationship would be a sin, rejects the notion that it would be wrong for a widow to remarry ("only in the Lord"), and rejects the notion that the slave should reconcile himself to a life of being a slave, even if he has an opportunity for manumission! Paul in fact says on the latter, "If you are given your opportunity for your legal freedom, go for it — remembering that your new status in Christ is what defines you." (2) Paul wrote this whole chapter in response to a letter from the Corinthians raising issues about sexuality in Christ. In all of this, Bartchy is right on target. Paul is not an ascetic, nor the son of an ascetic. He does not think that sexual relationships between married persons are inherently defiling. If anything he thinks the opposite — they might be sanctifying! It follows from all of this that 1 Corinthians 7 should cease being used to justify sub-Christian views of the goodness of human sexuality, or sub-Christian views of the goodness of human sexual relationships in proper moral contexts, or non-Pauline views of Paul, as if he were an ascetic. No one is encouraged to be an ascetic in 1 Corinthians 7. And finally, (3) nothing is said here or elsewhere in the whole New Testament that suggests celibacy is somehow an inherently more holy condition than being married, or that ministers or priests, if they are really serious about being holy or being called into the ministry, must dedicate themselves to celibacy, *whether or not they have the* charisma *for it.*

The Purpose and Limits of Sexual Relationships from a Kingdom Perspective

In our sex-obsessed culture, it is easy enough to make too much of sexual relations. And there are many, many studies done by able Christian counselors and psychologists on the matter. It is not the purpose of this section of the chapter to repeat what has been said in the voluminous literature on the subject, but rather to ask and answer one question: How should sexual relations be viewed in light of the Kingdom that is coming?

We have already noted that just as there will be no marrying and giving in marriage in the Kingdom, there will also likely be no sexual intercourse either, although at least one early Jewish rabbi said that "in the resurrection women will give birth daily to children" — a truly androcentric perspective on what bliss would look like in the Kingdom! Why no sex in the Kingdom? It is not because there is anything unholy about it, but because sexual intercourse was set up by God for several interrelated and specific this-worldly purposes: (1) the propagation of the species; (2) the bonding of husband and wife in a one-flesh union; (3) to enhance the pleasure and joy of fulfilling the creation order mandate and doing one's conjugal duty or privilege.

A moment's reflection will show that if we have everlasting resurrection bodies in the Kingdom, we certainly do not have mortality to fear any longer. The propagation of the species served the purpose of keeping mortal humans still extant on the earth since they were all the time being born and dying. This purpose no longer exists for sexual intercourse in the Kingdom. What about the second purpose? Since disease, decay, and death, suffering, sin, and sorrow, alienation, loneliness, and anxiety will be gone in the Kingdom, all the usual impediments to union and communion between persons will be removed. The union between humans and God, and humans and each other, will be so profound that it will transcend and make otiose sexual intercourse. An even greater sort and source of ecstasy and joy and bonding will be our daily delight — we will live right in the presence of a God who is love, and will never again doubt that we are loved, never again feel unloved, never feel a need for a rebonding, as we will never feel *apart* from each other anymore. With the creation order mandate obsolete and marriage left behind, and purpose and pure pleasure coming from other more divine sources, the third purpose of intercourse will also be superseded by something even more wonderful.

When one really begins to reflect on future Kingdom life, it casts a long shadow back on life in this age, in this vale of tears. It helps us understand why Paul would say that from now on, Christians should live "as if not," with a certain detachment from all the earthly institutions and purely earthly goods and joys we experience here. The point is, the joys of this age are only foretastes of glory divine, foreshadowings of the better life in the Kingdom. They are earthly institutions for our earthly good. They are not ends in themselves, nor are they means to those ends. By the latter remark I mean that marriage and intercourse and having children are not means of salvation or tickets into the Kingdom. 1 Timothy 2:15 should not be translated "and the woman shall be saved by childbearing"! Paul did not believe in justification by baby-making, even for women. That verse should either be translated "but woman shall be saved by the Childbearing" (that is, Mary reverses the curse brought about by Eve), or less likely "but woman shall be kept safe during childbearing" (again reversing the curse of labor pain and danger in labor on Eve).

All of this prompts a discussion of the limits imposed on human sexual expression in the New Testament in this age. In our own sex-crazed and sexually confused age, and considering human beings' infinite capacity for self-justification, all sorts of unbiblical ideas about marriage and what constitutes good sexual relating are being advocated, even within the church in some quarters. What we have already said here will help us in understanding something of the divinely imposed limits on sexual expression in the Bible.

The first point to be made is that since propagating the species was the original and indeed primary reason for giving all sorts of creatures the ability to copulate, any relationships that by their inherent nature cannot potentially produce the fruit of the womb are in fact not sanctioned in the Bible, and even some relationships that could produce offspring (such as that between the angels and human women in Gen. 6:1-4) are forbidden by God. God apparently does not want the creation-order relationships he set up in the beginning violated, either by crossing the boundaries between orders of creations (angels and humans, humans and animals) or, even within a particular species, by engaging in sexual activity that could never help replenish the species.

If we examine closely Genesis 1–2, and then later the way Jesus uses the creation order to undergird proper marriage in Matthew 19:1-12, it becomes clear why there is no sanction at all in the Bible for gay or lesbian sexual relationships: (1) they cannot be fruitful and so they do not serve the primary function of sexual intercourse, and (2) they violate the creation order in some way. God did not create just men or just women; rather, the story is that woman was specifically created for the man, Adam. This theological point cannot be gainsaid by claiming that God made person X or Y some other way, so that they were born inclined in another direction. In the first place, there is no biblical or for that matter scientific genetic evidence (say of a "gay gene") for such a claim. That is a modern myth.[22]

Imagine indeed if God had made primitive humans so that they were only attracted to their own gender and refused to sexually relate to the opposite sex. That species of creatures would have died out in a single generation before the rise of modern genetic engineering, sperm donating, and the like. It would have been singularly bad planning on God's part if God wanted human beings, created in his image, both male and female, to fulfill the mandate of actually filling the earth and subduing it. In fact, only men and women are capable of sharing a one-flesh union as described in the New Testament, and that phrase is used only of male-female sexual relating in the New Testament, for *neither Jesus nor Paul is simply talking about sexual intercourse; they are talk-*

---

22. On this whole matter one should consult R. Gagnon, *The Bible and Homosexual Practice* (Nashville: Abingdon, 2002).

The Rest of Life

ing about intercourse that leads to a union that bonds the two persons into one, a complex unity capable of bearing human fruit. They are talking about a union that should be shared only in the context of unconditional love, unconditional trust, until death parts them. They are talking about a union that should be shared only within the context of heterosexual monogamy.

The proof that this is so is everywhere to be found in the New Testament, not just in the passages where same-sex sexual sharing is seen as a sin (Romans 1; 1 Cor. 6:9; etc.), but in the passages that actually deal with both marriage and singleness. Take, for example, what Jesus says about these two states in Matthew 19:1-12. Jesus here is countering the argument of the Pharisees about grounds for divorce. He says quite clearly, "at the beginning the Creator made them male and female" (not male and male, or female and female), "and said 'for this reason a man will leave his father and mother and be joined to his wife, and the two will become one flesh.' So they are no longer two, but one. Therefore what God has joined together, let no one put asunder."

God here is seen as the one who brings the man and the woman together, and this is a clear allusion to Genesis 2:22-23, where God acts as the matchmaker, bringing the woman who has been fashioned out of the rib of the man, to the man. Jesus' teaching is that not just any sort of sexual relationships or coupling is an instance of where "God has joined them together." To the contrary, God only joins together the man and the woman. It is a corollary of this, of course, that plenty of people along the way, including various heterosexuals, have joined themselves together without God's leading or guidance, but if God did not join them together, it is not a marriage in God's eyes. This is the precise reason for the exception clauses in Matthew 5 and 19. The exception is for *porneia*, which both here and in 1 Corinthians 5 and elsewhere likely means incest. Jesus is alluding to the *cause célèbre* of his day — the incestuous relationship of Herod Antipas with his brother's wife. Jesus' cousin, John the Baptizer, lost his head for criticizing this incestuous relationship. Jesus is saying "no divorce" except when a relationship is entered into that is not a God-sanctioned or God-ordained marriage in the first place.

The disciples understandably go ballistic when the implications of this "no divorce" for God-sanctioned marital relations sinks in. They say, "If that is the way it is between a man and a woman, it's better not to marry." Jesus has just taken from the males their exclusive privilege of divorce in that patriarchal society, and they are ticked off. Jesus then quietly tells them, if they can't endure that stricture, then they have one other choice — celibacy for the sake of the Kingdom, a state Jesus uses the metaphor of the eunuch to describe, making clear that this other condition involves *no sexual sharing whatsoever,* for the eunuch was incapable of intercourse. Thus Jesus initiates what Paul reaffirms: Christians have two choices — marriage between a man and a woman, or remaining single for the sake of the Kingdom. Only these two choices would honor not only the creation order in which marriage is grounded and the creation-order mandate, but also where the Kingdom is going. The person who remains single in Christ in a sense foreshadows the eschatological time when there will be no more marrying and giving in marriage and no more sexual intercourse.

It is striking that in Isaiah 56:4-5 we hear about an eschatological promise of a day when, unlike in the times of the first temple, a eunuch will not be prohibited from entering and worshiping and being blessed in the house of God: "For this is what the Lord says: I will bless those eunuchs who keep my Sabbath days holy and who choose to do what pleases me and commit their lives to me. I will give them — within the walls of my house — a memorial and a name far greater than sons and daughters could give. For the name I give them is an everlasting one. It will never disappear!"

It is the rise of the goodness of singleness for the Lord that is the new thing we see in the person and the ministry of Jesus as a clear sign of the eschatological or Kingdom age and what life will be like in the Kingdom. 1 Corinthians 7 and Paul's teaching on *charisma* is just a further repristinizing of this eschatological vision and promise, a vision already partially coming to pass in persons like Paul who remained single for the sake of mission and ministry for Christ. It is not surprising, in light of all this, that we hear in 1 Timothy 3 about requirements that a minister limit the number of marital relationships he has. We should consider this passage at some length, since it has been often mistranslated and misinterpreted. Here is a fresh rendering:

> It is necessary then that the overseer be unimpeachable, a one-woman man, sober, temperate, well behaved, hospitable to strangers, having the gift of teaching, not addicted to wine, not pugnacious/contentious, but rather considerate, peaceable, not a money lover, a good supervisor of his own household, having children in order with all seriousness (but if anyone does not know how to supervise his own household, how can he look after the assembly of God?). He should not be a neophyte in order that he not be conceited, falling into the condemnation of the Diabolical One. But it is necessary also that he have a good reputation with the outsiders, in order that he not fall into disgrace and the snare of the Diabolical One.
>
> Likewise deacons inspiring respect, not double talkers, not addicted to much wine, not greedy, having hold of the mystery of the faith in a clean conscience. And these must be tested first, then serve as deacons, being irreproachable, women [deacons] likewise inspiring respect, not slanderers, sober, faithful in all. A deacon must be a one-woman man, supervising his children and household well, for those serving well are standing themselves in good stead to also acquire plentiful free speech in the faith which they have in Christ Jesus.

One of the more interesting aspects of this passage is that it is mostly a character description of the kind of person who can and ought to be a minister, not a job description per se. It will be worth exegeting this section in some detail here, as the whole issue of sexuality and ministry has raised serious questions about who can and cannot be ordained based on sexual orientation. Here it is stressed that the person in question must be of unimpeachable character. The Greek adjective *anepilempton* is also later applied to widows and to Timothy himself (1 Tim. 5:7; 6:14). It has to do with observable conduct that cannot be reproached. This seems to be the general moral heading for all the rest of the virtues yet to mentioned.

The meaning of the phrase *mias gunaikos aner,* which we also find at Titus 1:6 and the female equivalent at 1 Timothy 5:9, has been debated. Does it mean a man who has only one woman at a time (i.e., serial monogamy)? Does it mean a man who is not a polygamist or profligate or a homosexual? Does it mean a man who has been faithful to one woman throughout his life and so only married once? Does it make marriage a requirement for being an elder? Does it simply refer to marital faithfulness in an exclusively monogamous relationship?

It is unlikely that polygamy or polyandry is in view here, since this was not a regular practice in the Greco-Roman world (some eastern royalty being the exception). It is also unlikely that what is being said here is that a person *must* be married in order to be an elder, since that makes 1 Timothy 5:9 a tautology, plus the emphatic position of the word "one" in the Greek phrase is strongly against the idea that what is being stressed here is the need for a married rather than a single man. This narrows down the options considerably.

The ancient inscriptional evidence where we find women lauded for being *univira* and *monandros* on epitaphs, by which was meant women and men who did not remarry after their spouse died, has been used to point to the conclusion that Paul is speaking of those who have only been married once in a lifetime (ruling out marriage after divorce as well as after the demise of the spouse). The problem with this view is that in 1 Corinthians 7 Paul says that widows may remarry, only in the Lord, though his preference would be for such folks to remain single as he is for the sake of the Dominion.

It is furthermore often overlooked that the *univira* inscription is about a woman who did not remarry after the mentioned spouse died. It says nothing about whether she had been previously married, and remarriage in any case was not seen as sinful or culturally unacceptable in that world. If one studies the matter closely, what is being praised in those inscriptions is a sort of exceptional devotion of a woman to her deceased husband, and in a patriarchal world celibacy after the death of a partner was seen as a virtue for a woman but was not expected of men.[23] Furthermore, neither the male nor female Greek phrases we are concerned with are used in those Latin inscriptions that refer to the *univira.* Nearer to the mark is the epigram of Carphyllides from the second century B.C., which reads *mies apelausa gynaikos* — "I enjoyed one wife, who grew old with me" (*Greek Anthology* 7.260). The idea there is restricting oneself to one woman, which points us in the right direction for our text.

In the Pastorals themselves there is the further problem that in 1 Timothy 5:14 young widows are actually encouraged to remarry, so it seems unlikely at least in 1 Timothy 5:9 that the phrase means married only once in a lifetime, unless the Pastorals are enunciating one standard for elders and another for others (are young widows an especial exception to a "once only" rule?).

Here is where we note the strong stress in this passage on being morally irreproachable. It is therefore far more likely that what the phrase in question is dealing with is behavior *within*

23. See the discussion in C. W. Emmet, "The Husband of One Wife," *Expository Times* 19 (1907-8): 39-40; J. B. Frey, "La signification des termes *monandros* et *univira*," *Recherche de science religieuse* 20 (1930): 48-60; M. Lightman and W. Zeisel, "Univira: An Example of Continuity and Change in Roman Society," *Church History* 46 (1977): 19-32; S. Page, "Marital Expectations of Church Leaders in the Pastoral Epistles," *Journal for the Study of the New Testament* 50 (1993): 105-20.

marriage, which is to say, being sexually faithful to one's own wife, and so not engaging in any sort of extramarital infidelity. In other words, the double standard in regard to sexual ethics that existed for married men and women in the Greco-Roman world is being ruled out. Unlike a prohibition of polygamy, which was widely condemned in that culture, this teaching would be a new restriction for some. For our purposes, what is stressed is that the elder has his libido under control, and it assumes that a moral marriage only involves one man and one woman.

It also becomes clear with verse 5 that one of the undergirding assumptions here is that a person who cannot manage his own household certainly should not be entrusted with the task of managing the household of God. Here we are told that an elder should have believing (or faithful?) children rather than children who could be accused of extravagance and insubordination; another way to translate it is, not wasteful or headstrong. This criterion assumes that the children are well into adolescence, if not beyond it.

This general description of the elder simply assumes that the persons in question will be married, just as it assumes they will have children, since both of these were the norm in that society, and it explains what an overseer's behavior must be like as a married person with children. He must be faithful to his *one* (the position of the word "one" is emphatic) wife, forsaking all others. Paul has nothing against widows or widowers remarrying after the death of the spouse, as 1 Timothy 5:14 makes evident.

The character description of the overseer stresses five vices to avoid and six virtues to be cultivated in addition to being faithful to one's spouse. In verse 2b it is said that this person must be sober (cf. 2 Tim. 4:5), temperate, well behaved, hospitable ("friendly to strangers"; see Rom. 12:13; 1 Peter 4:9; 1 Clement 1:2; Did. 11-12; Aristides, *Apology* 15; Epictetus, *Discourses* 1.28.23), not a drunkard or addicted to much wine (perhaps with an echo of Lev. 10:8-9). Neither here nor at verse 8, nor at 1 Timothy 5:23 nor at Titus 1:7, is the reference to total abstinence or teetotaling by church leaders, as 1 Timothy 5:23 makes very clear, though there the reference is to a medicinal use of wine.

The condemnation here of greediness is perhaps in part due to the fact that this seems to have been a trait of the false teachers (1 Tim. 6:3-5; 2 Tim. 2:22-26). There is a stress here, unlike what we find in Titus 1, on the overseer having the "gift/aptitude for teaching" (see also 2 Tim. 2:24), not merely holding fast to teaching passed down to him (see 1 Tim. 5:17). This is perhaps in part because the false teachers posed a more serious problem already in Ephesus than on Crete.

In addition, the overseer is not to be pugnacious (literally, not a striker/giver of blows) but rather considerate, peaceable, and not avaricious. It was a regular phenomenon in Paul's world that people (philosophers, teachers, rhetors) taught for money, and the avaricious speaker or teacher was regularly parodied (cf. Philostratus, *Life of Apollonius of Tyana* 1.34; Dio Chrysostom, *Orations* 32.9, 11; 35.1; Lucian, *The Runaways* 14; *Philosophies for Sale* 24). The danger always was that the teacher might customize the teaching to put someone in a trance or tickle the fancy of the audience just so he might be paid. This was perhaps somewhat less of a problem for nonitinerant teachers who had a stable source of income — for instance, as the teacher in the house of a noble patron. It is not, however, a coincidence that Paul juxtaposes here in this list "the gift of teaching" with "not a lover of money."

Verse 4 stresses the principle that if someone can't "manage" their own household they should not be allowed to manage or supervise the household of God (cf. 1 Tim. 5:7). The children of the overseer must be "in order" or submissive with all seriousness or respect. Notice that nothing is said about forcing them to submit, but rather it is assumed that the conduct of the family life will be such that the children will be encouraged and even want to behave.

Here in this passage we also have this notion that believers have been formed into a family or household, which requires supervision and guidance and which belongs to God. Frequently there are analogies in the Pastorals drawn between behavior in the physical family and its household and the household of God, which is of course natural since the two entities overlapped and congregated in the same space of someone's home. It needs to be stressed then that Paul is not just talking about what we would call behavior "in church" or in a church meeting, but rather behavior by those who are members of the household of God. Chrysostom once made the comment that "the Church is, as it were, a small household" *(Homily 10 on 1 Timothy).* But it was more than just a microcosm of the family structure, as its leadership requirements show. Further, here and in 5:3-16 it is perfectly clear that Paul does not dissolve the boundaries between the household and the household of God, so that there is little distinction between the two.

In verse 6 we hear the requirement that this person should not be a novice, or to transliterate, a "neophyte" (the term literally means newly planted; cf. LXX Ps. 127:3; 143:12; Isa. 5:7; Job 14:9). This certainly refers to a new convert; it may even refer to someone newly baptized, and we must notice a difference here from what is found in Titus 1, where there may have been no choice but to appoint neophytes as elders in some cases. The church in Ephesus was a more well-established one.

Even if we are only talking about Pauline house churches, if this letter is written in the mid-60s then there will have been churches founded by Paul or one of his co-workers here for at least ten years. The thought here is that people who move up the leadership ladder too fast may become conceited (*tuphousthai* literally means to be filled with smoke, elsewhere in the New Testament only at 1 Tim. 6:4 and 2 Tim. 3:4) and fall into the condemnation of the Devil (literally "the Slanderer"; see 2 Tim. 2:26). This may mean fall under the judgment the Devil himself fell under because of his pride and arrogance, or it may mean fall into a condemnation the Devil would bring and pronounce on a person, though elsewhere the Devil is depicted as slanderer and an accuser of believers (see Job 1–2), but not as a judge. This very term is used to describe the false teachers in 1 Timothy 6:4 and 2 Timothy 3:4, which not only suggests that these descriptions have one eye on the flaws of the false teachers, but also suggests that some of the false teachers were already "high" authorities within the church, perhaps elders, and perhaps indeed they were aspiring to be overseers. If so, Paul is nipping that problem in the bud here.

Verse 7 indicates the necessity of having a good reputation with non-Christians, so that one will not fall into public disgrace, thereby disgracing the church in the eyes of potential converts, and thus fall into a snare of the Devil who is constantly trying to make the church look bad in the world's eyes. The main point seems to be that the Devil is more successful at catching novices in his snare, so Christian leaders should be experienced people. One suspects that the reason for mentioning this is precisely because of the false teachers who were indeed leaders in the house churches, and perhaps were relatively young in the faith, and had fallen into the specified trap, being both arrogant and ignorant, a bad combination. There may also be the thought that discrediting the church in the eyes of the world is one of the Devil's main ruses or traps (see 2 Tim. 2:26).

It is clear that the Pastorals show concern for the public face of Christianity, especially as would be reflected in its most visible and well-known members — usually high-status Christians. What we get no sense of in these letters is that the church in Ephesus was already dealing with persecution from without. The problems seem to be entirely internal, false Christian teachers and immature Christians in general being the main issues. On the whole, this material certainly does not sound like what we hear in Revelation 2–3, written to this area in the 90s, much less what we hear in Ignatius of Antioch's letters. The church in Ephesus is not yet a target, indeed not yet in a significant way on the radar screen of pagans; hence it is possible to just concentrate here on the need to be a good public witness. The hope is that more converts can be gained in this fashion.

Once again we have the word "likewise" at verse 8, and thus we realize that deacons are to meet the same sort of character requirements as overseers. The only noticeable differences are (1) the teaching function of overseers is not repeated; (2) hospitality is not mentioned as the deacon's function; (3) they are to be "tested." Surely the overseers were to be tested as well, unless we are to think that overseers would rise through the ranks, first serving as deacons before becoming overseers.

The meaning of "tested" in verse 10 seems to be that a person has a probationary period in office, or perhaps it just means a seasoned or veteran Christian. In addition, deacons are to inspire respect, and they are not to be two-faced or, better translated, "double-talkers." The need for authenticity and consistency of walking what one talks is implied, and duplicity especially is being ruled out. They also are not to be given to too much wine, are not to be greedy, and they must hold the "mystery of faith" in a clean conscience. Notice that of the nine traits or virtues of the deacon, six are directly parallel to that of the overseer. It is also striking that the deacon is nowhere said to be under the authority of the overseer. Paul is not really concerned about laying out a detailed leadership schematic or power structure here, much less institutionalizing the assembly and its leadership.

The term *mysterion* refers to something once obscure, unknown, or hidden that has now been revealed. A likely translation of the phrase is "the revealed truth" (cf. 1 Cor. 2:1, 7; 4:1; Eph. 3:3-9). It seems to refer to the salvation available to us as revealed in and through Christ. Not only must the deacon then be clear and clearly affirm with a good conscience the heart of the faith, but also he must be tested first before he serves as a deacon. This may suggest a careful examination of someone's life rather than a probationary period in office. The main thing to be discerned is the person's character and whether it is beyond reproach. The vision of ministry in this passage is rather similar to what we find in 1 Corinthians 2–4, especially when Paul says in 4:1 that he and others are household stewards of the mysteries of God.

Verse 11 also begins with the word "likewise" or "in like manner." There is much debate about whether we have a parenthetical comment here about the wives of deacons, or deaconesses. It could be either, but grammatically this sentence is dependent on verse 2 and the verb "must," just as verse 8 was dependent on it, so we would expect a continued discussion about church functionaries. But if it is deacons' wives, it is hard to imagine Paul not making the same comments about the wives of the overseers and indeed making that comment first. Paul is not dealing here with a household code, ordering the various members of the family as in Colossians 3–4 or Ephesians 5–6. He is dealing with leaders within the household of God, as he makes clear. We may contrast what is said here with what is said about the women who are out of line in 1 Timothy 2:11-15 and 2 Timothy 3:6-7. What I am suggesting is that Paul is positively comparing overseers, deacons, and deaconesses, but he is doing a rhetorical *synkrisis* or contrast with the false teachers and misbehaving women that are discussed elsewhere in this document and in 2 Timothy.

The word *gunaikas* literally means woman, not deaconess; as Romans 16:1 will show, where Phoebe is called a "deacon," there was no female equivalent noun yet in Greek for such a person. Pliny (*Epistles* 10.96) mentions two Christian female *ministrae* or deaconesses in the early second century in this general region, and there it seems to be something of a technical term. I thus conclude that it is likely to refer to deaconesses, since Paul elsewhere does mention such folks. What a careful study of passages like this shows is that (1) a particular gender is not a prerequisite for ministry in Christ, and (2) the Old Testament priesthood is not the pattern or paradigm or job description for ministers in Christ.

Verse 12 returns to the male deacons after the parenthesis and is a repetition of what was required for the overseer. Verse 13, however, offers something new — "for those serving well as deacons acquire a good standing for themselves and free speech in faith in Christ Jesus." The word *bathmos* occurs only here in the New Testament and means either base, foundation, or stair, or standing or rank. It is probably the latter in this case. The reference could be about one obtaining a higher standing in the church and so being a candidate for promotion, so to speak, to overseer if one serves well. Or it is possible that what is meant is just that someone obtains a good reputation by such service with recognition for it, thus improving their honor rating. The outcome of such faithful service is that one also has more confidence or assurance in the faith and in Christ (see Eph. 3:12, or one could read the concluding clause to mean that one has the right to speak freely about the faith and Christ, *parresia* often having the sense of bold or free speech; see Philemon v. 8). The list of requirements ends here without telling us what the structure of the community leadership will be.

Nothing is said about the relationship between overseers and deacons. Further, we can only guess at the scope of the work of each one since what we have is primarily character descriptions rather than job descriptions. As Chrysostom once said: "The blessed Paul, as though painting some royal likeness, and furnishing an original sketch of it having mixed the different colors of virtue, has painted in the features of the office of *episkopos,* in order that each who aspire to that dignity, looking upon the sketch, may administer their own affairs with just such strictness" *(Homily 2 on St. Ignatius and St. Babylas).* I would underline the word "sketch."

I have spent some time on the details of this passage because in one sense it sums up all the attributes of a Christian that we have discussed in each of the chapters in this book and the other books in this series. The minister is to be a good example in the way he or she worships, works, rests, manages money, manages his household, eats, drinks, studies, and teaches, and of course in his or her

The Rest of Life

character. The only characteristic not mentioned directly or indirectly in 1 Timothy 3 or Titus 1 is the importance of play.

Paul assumes that leaders will lead by example, as he assumes that their example will be followed, for better or worse. As Chaucer put it when speaking about priests and the effect of their witness on the congregation, "If gold rust, what then shall iron do? For if the priest be bad, in whom we trust, what wonder is it if a layman rust?" What this priest would say to us, and what Paul does say to us, is that in these sexually confused and sex-obsessed times, it is all the more crucial that ministers especially express their sexuality in the appropriate biblical ways — being "one-woman men," or "one-man women," or remaining single and celibate for the sake of the Kingdom. These are the options Jesus presented to his original disciples, and they are also the only options presented to us.

And So?

It is not the task of the church to baptize the ever-changing mores of human society and call them good. It is rather our task to be faithful to the gospel in all ages, faithful to the Word of God whether we worship or sleep, work or rest, whether we play or contemplate, whether we eat or conjugate the verb "to love." In all of the normal activities of a normal Christian life we are called to see all things in the light of Christ behind us, Christ before us, and Christ beside us. We must also live our lives in this age with one eye on the horizon, letting the eschatological light of the Kingdom reflect back on how we view the normal activities of life, and allowing that light to transfigure and transform both the way we think about all these normal activities of life, and the way we act when we carry out these activities. The clarion cry of Paul is that we remember that the eschatological clock is ticking, and that the forms of this world and all its institutions are passing away. Therefore we must sit lightly with all these things, seeing them as but foreshadowings and foretastes of the good things yet to come. We must live "as if not," not making mere means into ends in themselves. All things have been relativized in Christ. There is no more Jew or Gentile, slave or free, no male and female, for all are one in Christ (Gal. 3:28).

What this detachment does for us all is that it makes space for us to make "the main thing, the main thing" — namely, our everlasting union and communion with God in Christ and his people, which begins now and continues in eternity. The full embrace of God requires that we unclench our fists and be generous, not turn our fellow humans into idols (even American idols), and not take our work, or play or rest or study or eating or drinking or sexual expression, as the most important things in our lives. There is, as Pascal said, a God-shaped vacuum in every human soul, which only God can fill. And there is a human need in those created in God's image, which only God can satisfy. And one day when we see face to face we will have all that we need, and want only what we have. Until then —

"To him who is able to keep you from stumbling and present you before his glorious presence without fault and with great joy" . . . keep your hearts and minds in Christ Jesus. "May the God of peace who through the blood of the eternal covenant brought back from the dead our Lord Jesus, that great Shepherd of the sheep, equip you with every good thing for doing his will, and may he work in us what is pleasing to him through Jesus Christ, to whom be glory, forever and ever. Amen."[24]

24. A combination of the doxology in Jude and the benediction at the end of Hebrews.

CHAPTER SIX

As for the Rest of Life . . .

If there is one thing that almost all the volumes in this series have in common, it is that we are dealing with subjects that, strangely enough, seldom get detailed theological or ethical discussion from a biblical point of view. Oh yes, there is still plenty of debate about sabbatarian practice, but hardly any discussion of ordinary rest and its importance to the Christian life. We have already noted the paucity of any kind of discussion of a theology or ethic of play, and oddly the same thing can be said about study. And yet the Bible repeatedly exhorts believers to study. Nor do theologians and ethicists discuss food and eating from a biblical perspective much, though goodness knows there is plenty about food in the Bible, even food miraculously provided by God or Jesus. And even when we get to sex, the discussion tends to be so psychologized or secularized, or discussed from a counseling perspective, that hardly any serious attention is given to an eschatological or Kingdom perspective on the matter. It is this latter that we have attempted to bring to all these various subjects.

When we consider the normal daily Christian life of work and rest, worship and·study, play and eating, sex and relating, some thought should be given as to how to keep all these things in proper perspective and in some equilibrium. It's no help, for example, to have a balanced diet and have some sort of imbalance in the amount of rest or play or study or sex we are engaging in. I am not suggesting we follow the motto "all things in moderation," though that would be a pretty good motto if the subject were just eating and resting and working and studying and having sex, but in fact the problem is that most of us need to increase several of these activities and do less of others. In many cases, we need to eat less, and sleep more. We certainly need to worship and fellowship more, and we probably need to work less and spend more time with family and church friends. It is difficult to juggle all the aspects of life and keep all of the balls in the air at once.

There is something to be said for taking a "seasons of life" approach to some of this. For example, my season in life for playing basketball or running marathons is over. It's too hard on the ankles and knees these days. So instead I jog and walk nine holes of golf each week, in tandem with mowing my lawn once a week with a push mower; that's all the exercise my nearly sixty-year-old body will bear these days. As Kenny Rogers said, "You gotta know when to hold them, know when to fold them, know when to walk away. . . ." You catch my drift. When it comes to diet and exercise you have to listen to what your body is telling you and behave sensibly, especially if you have a family or people depending on you financially.

I am not suggesting, however, that we should plan our lives so that in the winter of life we are basically useless, doing nothing important for the Kingdom of God. I don't believe in being a workaholic, but I don't believe retirement is a biblical notion either. One may retire from one's secular vocation, but if so, then it's time for more volunteer work at the Salvation Army or at the church, or around town in various ways. As Mr. Wesley used to say, you now have time for more works of piety and charity. Consider that your new vocation.

There is of course also a season in life for having children, raising them, sending them off to school, and then adjusting to an empty nest. And as one gets older one has to adjust to the changes in one's body and that of one's mate as well. Sometimes this means less sex, and sometimes it even means no more sex. That doesn't mean there can't still be love and intimacy. Sex is not the be-all and end-all of real love and intimacy, though you would never know that these days from all the Viagra commercials. From a Kingdom perspective we know that, even in regard to sex, the day is coming that "this too shall pass." For some it comes a little sooner than for others, and guess what — it's not the end of the world! Indeed, it is precisely because there is a good end that the world is tending to that we won't need a lot of things that we need now in this temporal age. We do need work and making a living, we do need sex and offspring, we do need rest and study and play and eating here and now to keep living a normal life.

But the day is coming when we will not need all of the current necessities of ongoing life. And this is precisely why Paul says in regard to this age's necessities that we live with some detachment, that we live "as if not," because the form and institutions of this world are indeed becoming obsolete. If we learn the secret of sitting lightly with the things of this life, our own mental and emotional worlds will not collapse if, for example, we lose our job, or our spouse, or some of our physical abilities. What did Cat Stevens say in the song "Moonshadow"? "And if I ever lose my hands, lose my power, lose my land . . . Ooh, I won't have to work no more."

The one thing we must not lose, the one thing we must make the main thing is not work or rest or play or sexual relations, or eating or study, but rather our worship and our relationship with the Lord. Love never fails and never ends, and in particular the love relationship we have with God never ends. All other things are relative goods and may come and go. Only the church's relationship with its Bridegroom is everlasting. If we have this Kingdom perspective on life, all will be well, and all manner of things will be well, even when all is not going well, humanly speaking.

Sometimes we as Christians make the mistake of making

something less than God the object of our ultimate concern — whether it is a spouse, or children, or work, or even other things. When we do this, and that object of ultimate concern leaves or dies or grows up, we find ourselves without meaning and purpose in our lives. Whether we realize it or not, what we have done is committed a subtle form of idolatry, allowing something less than God to be God in our lives, or our object of ultimate concern. My hope would be that through this series of books, we would gain perspective on what our true calling in life is — to love God and enjoy him forever — and that we would see with Kingdom eyes all these other aspects of life that confront us day after day.

We need both perspective, and a plan for the seasons of life when it comes to work, rest, play, study, eating, and sex. We need to be able to make midcourse corrections all along the way. Life is all about adjustments. Just when you think you've gotten into a good groove, you find yourself in a rut, and it's time for a change. In a temporal and temporary world of space and time, there is nothing as permanent as change. Only the Lord is a fixed point in this turning world, which is why we should fix our gaze on him above all else. What is it that the hymn says? "Turn your eyes upon Jesus, look full in his wonderful face, and the things of this world will grow strangely dim, in the light of his wonder and grace."

I would put it a little differently: in the light of the Kingdom and in the light of Christ, we can see things for what they really are — temporary blessings and opportunities. Work and rest and play and study and eating and sex are temporary blessings and opportunities. And as long as we don't put the emphasis on the wrong syllable and make them objects of ultimate concern, we can enjoy them for what they are — things given to us for our temporal good, so we may be of use and service to God and others in this life.

There is, however, one more mile we must go in these explorations. We must consider what "normal" spiritual formation should look like, in light of all these other factors. In what ways can all these things be done to the glory of God and for the edification of ourselves and others? In the final book in this series, we will deal with what a reasoned and reasonable approach to the spiritual formation of all life should look like for a Christian. Remember the famous quote from Ecclesiastes?

There is a time for everything,
and a season for every activity under heaven:
a time to be born and a time to die,
a time to plant and a time to uproot,
a time to kill and a time to heal,
a time to tear down and a time to build,
a time to weep and a time to laugh,
a time to mourn and a time to dance,
a time to scatter stones and a time to gather them,
a time to embrace and a time to refrain,
a time to search and a time to give up,
a time to keep and a time to throw away,
a time to tear and a time to mend,
a time to be silent and a time to speak,
a time to love and a time to hate,
a time for war and a time for peace.

I must take exception to this poem just a little bit in closing. There really isn't a time to hate other human beings. There really isn't a time for racism, for example, or for child abuse, for example, or for pornography. There really isn't a time for terrorism or murder if you are a Christian. There really isn't a time for adultery or slander. There isn't really a time for ever so many wicked and sinful things in life, yet they happen. There isn't a time for absolutely everything under heaven. But broadly speaking, the author is right. And keeping all of life in perspective and in equilibrium does involve having a sense of time and timing, and also a strong sense of what is and isn't timeless.

Yet, there are ways of living that do indeed prevent us from being open to serendipity, open to God doing a new thing in our lives, open to change. To one degree or another we are all creatures of habit, and sometimes we cling to our routines to give us a sense that life is orderly and all is well. It gives us a sense of security. But in fact, our faith and trust and security should be in the Lord, not in the orderly routines that are our ways of trying to keep life at bay, to control life. When we try to control our lives through set routines, we miss all sorts of opportunities presented to us by God.